Flawed to the Core:
Building Memorable Characters and Writing

By: Kyle Belote

Copyright Page

Initial edit by: J.C. Wing
https://www.wingfamilyediting.com

Book Cover by: Ivan Zanchetta © 2025
https://www.bookcoversart.com

Author Substack: https://www.outpostdire.com

Works By The Author

<u>The Dark Legacy Series:</u> (Grimdark Fantasy)
The Bearer of Secrets
Mark of the Profane
The Jackal of Shades

<u>The Maro Prakk Novella Series:</u> (Western Fantasy)
Red Creek
Bloodbane

<u>The Warmaster Series:</u> (Military Sci-fi Fantasy)
The Demon's Fate
Decimation Protocol (2026)

<u>Other Works:</u>
Flawed to the Core: Building Memorable Characters and Writing
The Dark Portal (Sci-fi Thriller)
For Heathens of Heaven (poetry)

Acknowledgements

To Sophie, thanks for the idea, being a pest about it, and making sure I got it done. Without you, this book would've never been written. So, in a way, everyone owes you a debt of gratitude.

Dedication

For Sophie.

Foreword from David Williamson

The carpenter does not come and say, "Hear me talk about the carpenter's art;" but having undertaken to build a house, he makes it, and proves that he knows the art.
—Epictetus in Discourses, book 3.

Writing a book about writing is a lofty goal.

When can one call themselves a writer? When can they deem themselves knowledgeable on the subject?

Many aspiring writers struggle so deeply with their internal editors and demons that they would never attempt such a thing. "What do I have to say about this? I barely know what I'm doing."

Even so, over time, diligence and discipline produce results that speak on one's behalf. Along the way, others start to ask questions, because they want similar success. "How did you get that done? What is your process? What secret have you figured out that I don't know yet? How do I learn to do what you are already doing?"

So it was for Kyle, and I am not surprised.

When I came to Okinawa in 2014, I left behind the first writing group I ever knew. I searched for a similar support system, and even tried to get some critique groups going, but to no avail.

After a dismal year or two, I found a local college professor hosting writing workshops and meetings on base, and I latched onto that opportunity.

Still, participation seemed sporadic, and every few weeks I wondered if it was worth the effort.

Then I met Kyle.

Here—finally!—was a fellow writer digging into the motivations that spur characters into noble or cruel actions, the importance of certain beats along the protagonist's journey, the value of the editing process and critiques from fellow readers, and so many other aspects of the craft.

Someone who got it.

Someone who cared.

Someone who challenged me to want to do better in my own effort.

Someone who not only called out my weak spots but offered helpful suggestions for how to make them stronger.

Over the next few years, Kyle and I traded chapters and characters, tore through paragraphs and plot lines, scrutinized sentences and scenes... and found companions on the journey.

A new librarian at the base wanted to start a writing community. "Well, you're in luck," Kyle said as we introduced ourselves and explained the group we had been running for months.

Two NaNoWriMo (National Novel Writing Month) participants stuck with the grueling nature of that one-month challenge and decided to jump into our critique group afterward. They became insightful friends with whom we could share and improve our own efforts for a couple years, and they brought along another aspiring writer.

We spent hours poring over pages while pouring cups of coffee, learning each other's creative styles as we experienced the fantastic settings inside their heads.

We took turns sharing our thoughts on different facets of writing, hoping that we could each expand the collection of tools and techniques in our kits.

We celebrated achievements and encouraged one another when life got in the way of the word count.

Through it all, Kyle kept plugging away, grinding out lengthy tomes, gritty and full of action, advancing the vision for several novels that he had been developing for years.

Kyle is not an arrogant carpenter proclaiming his knowledge or applauding his own art.

He is one who has built houses out of words—and living worlds around their written walls.

I've had the distinct pleasure of spending time in some of them, and I look forward to more.

Chapter 1: Introduction

Fair Warning

Everything you are about to read is coming from a pantser, a specific type of writer. If you're not a pantser, you may find kernels within that help you regardless. For those of you who are like me, this will show you how I build a story, world, and characters.

To everyone reading, I hope you find something for you.

I'll try to make this as streamlined as possible with no frills. You want to read something quick and engaging and learn. That's what I wish for you, too. So, without further ado...

Who This Book is For

If you are new to writing, this book is for you; if you're a writer who's been hanging around the block for a few years, dipping your toes into stories but haven't finished or completed a few works, you'll find this book helpful in many regards.

And for those who've been at it for a long time, this book will give you a new take on many elements you're already familiar with. You can skip to the sections you're interested in. For those who are new or novices, the book's emphasis will be characters, but the other chapters will guide you in other fundamentals you may be unfamiliar with. That said, I don't want to assume that everyone has a foundation.

Words to Live By

When I was in my teens, I saw an article about my favorite 90s band, the Smashing Pumpkins. Being a novice musician and an avid fan, I snatched up the magazine and peered within. I don't remember anything about the article, the magazine, the pictures, or the news. Only one thing stuck out to me, and still clings to me two decades later: a single quote from Billy Corgan—the singer and lead guitarist. I don't recall it verbatim, but the intent I'll paraphrase: "There is no wrong or right way to make music/a guitar riff." This was the staple of my music for many years; it's become a staple of my writing now.

Take these words literally, figuratively, and metaphorically: "There's no wrong or right way to write."

There isn't a template that says, "this is the way and only way." Writing is a freeing experience despite the shackle around your heart. You can create your characters first, or you can build your world, or any other point in the process. It's not like building a house, you don't have to have a slab and framework before starting your roof. The choice is yours on where to start, but we need to find what place is best for you.

But…

Does this mean everything you write will be a success? No. You will face countless failures and setbacks along the way, and the way you become a better writer is to learn from those failures. Failure is the backbone of success in every walk of life. The world would be a darker place if Thomas Edison gave up the first time his inventions failed. So, fail. Fail many times. Hit rock bottom, but pick yourself back up, and try again.

And then, write.

The Journey Begins

My creative writing journey began in 2003. I never wanted to be a writer, never thought it possible. At most, I read science fiction and *Star Wars Expanded Universe* novels. That was the extent of my soirée.

As cliché as it may sound by now, my first novel did come to me in a dream—a fevered one—the most realistic, lucid dream I'd ever had up to that point, and elements still come to me in 2020. I've never had another one like it. If you want to read the long story, you can visit my blog at https://www.outpostdire.com.

When I woke the next day, I began scribbling the story down on paper. It had to mean something, right? I wrote as much as I could until my hand cramped. The next day, I wrote more of what I remembered, expanding and fleshing out the details. The sentences turned to paragraphs, then the paragraphs turned to pages. Before long, I'd written almost fifty pages, longhand. Thus, my journey began.

Many folks, from what I've heard, started out this way. A dream, a situation, some clairvoyant moment that altered them forever. What was yours? Can you remember? Or perhaps you always knew you were meant to be an author. Maybe you started young with poetry and short stories as a child and graduated into a full-blown novelist. Or perhaps this is your first time. If so, welcome. To those who've been clacking away forever, make yourselves at home.

I never intended to write a self-help book on writing. With so many out there, it seems almost redundant at this point. From the few I've read, they tend to be more formulaic. I hope to deliver this one with a touch of personalization. Many things you read within are my own self-discovered kernels of … well, I won't say wisdom, but perhaps enlightenment.

Others are knickknacks I picked up over the years from friends or, at the very least, brainstorming sessions with folks who didn't mind talking about my book with me.

Whether you are published, self-published, or still in the crafting phase, you *are* a writer. Don't let anyone tell you differently. You must see yourself as one, envision your success—however that may turn out to be —and hold true to the path. The road is long, perilous, and will require more sacrifices than you can possibly imagine.

So, let's get started.

The Book's Focus

This book will focus on elements of writing such as writing tools, software for writing and self-editing, and others like:

Self-Preparation: Knowing your writer type—Pantser, Outliner, Snowflake Method, and Edit-as-you-Go. Setting your mood to write with music and canceling all distractions, or knowing your target audience before diving into other elements.

Preparing for the Story with Story Structure: The 5Ws, Three Acts, The LOCK Structure, Yes, but/No, and method, the Monomyth (Hero's Journey), Harmon's Circle, and my own approach.

World-Building: Why not settle for Earth, the Three Whys, other means of World Building, my own approach, and Asinine Questions to Avoid.

Character Building: Archetypes, Myers-Briggs, Enneagrams, and how I build characters.

Other Elements: Seven types of Conflict, Dialogue Tags, Dialogue, Action, Sex, what readers skip, prologues, and the like, and Self-Editing & Critiquing.

They say as long as your characters are fantastic, your reader will forgive you for not having a remarkable story. But if your tale is stellar and you have flat characters, nothing on Earth can save you.

What the book won't cover: what comes after you're done writing and self-editing, seeking an agent, or pursuing the traditional or self-publishing routes. This decision is for you to make, and there are a plethora of knowledgeable sources available when you wish to delve deeper into these aspects.

Hard Truths

Writing a book is much harder than the average person assumes. It's a long, mired process of brainstorming, crafting, creating, editing, crying, and doubting yourself. Then, the cycle repeats. I'm sure you've heard at one point or another, "I've thought about writing a book," or "I've written a book."

When I hear this, I fight my initial impulse to eye-roll, as many of you have. The ultimate irritant is when someone says, "Anyone can write a book." And yes, that's true. Anyone *can*, but will they? Going a step further, the question is: will it be any good? To this, I'd bet no ninety-seven percent of the time.

Fear not! There are ways you can combat the naysayers as they try to upstage you or bring their negativity, counter by asking these questions:

"Is it available for sale" / "Where can I buy it?"

"How many times did you revise before sending it to beta readers?"

"Who's your editor? Perhaps I can speak to them?"

"What publishing house did you end up with?"

"Can I read it?"

If delivered in a genuine tone, these simple, innocent questions should end all up-stagers, one uppers, and potential detractors. Don't let them heckle you. There will always be at least one. The point of the questions isn't to belittle them but rather show how serious you are as a writer.

When they don't have answers, you can go back to what you were doing as they slink away. Or, you may find that these questions lead you to a new, life-long friend and critique partner. This is why it's essential to ask in a genuine tone. Best not to burn bridges before they form.

Another hard truth that many discover along the way—though I'm not saying this is true for everyone: your family, your parents, brothers, sisters, or friends aren't going to read your work. If they do, count yourself lucky and blessed! I wish I had a family like yours. Also, they're biased. It's you, right? They wouldn't say anything too bad! And one last thing, just because they read your work doesn't mean it's their preferred genre. Take the critiques with a larger-than-normal helping of salt.

Here are some other hard truths to swallow. They don't warrant their own paragraphs, so we'll do it rapid-fire like.

- *Everyone "thought about writing"* until they were called out. I honestly believe most folks think this is a great conversation piece. Maybe they think it'll make them relate.
- *If you think you can't learn anything from critiques and beta readers, let alone editors, you need a wake-up call.* Learning is continuous.
- *There's no such thing as a perfect manuscript on the first try.* Even famous authors revise, and yes, they have editors—a team of them in most cases.

11

- *If you think you can skip the editor or beta readers because you know a lot about grammar—or your buddies do—don't be surprised when no one reads or slams your book in reviews after you self-publish.* This, above all, is paramount. Don't skip the beta reader phase. Don't skip an editor! Readers—consumers—are vicious! They expect a level of quality, and when you self-publish, it's presumed that you deliver a polished, edited story. Moreover, as they're ripping apart your work, don't expect a level of professionalism. They'll espouse their views loudly and often. Unfortunately, they don't hold traditionally published authors to the same standards. So ... GET. AN. EDITOR! There are many types, and you need to be sure which you need if you're on a budget. We'll cover this in Chapter 7.
- *You're at the end of your first draft. Guess what? That was the easy part.*
- *If you receive feedback from beta readers or critiquers and your first response is they're wrong, it's time to do some real soul searching.*
- *When you start to think your writing is incredible, but you've never faced critiquers, it's time to rip that Band-Aid off.*

So, how long is it going to take for you to become a competent writer? If you're looking for a quick and easy path, a formula to calculate, or a definitive time frame, you won't find one. It's all on you. Yes, many things can aid and speed you on your way, but I didn't have that until later in my journey. So, we'll learn the hard way.

I once heard the first million words you write are just the surface of learning the craft. To this, I agree. I've written a million. By now, probably two to two-and-a-half million. And I'm still learning. There isn't a finish line to cross; there's only the next craft. How many have you written? And yes, rewrites count. In rewriting, you learn. And that's what the end goal should be: to learn, evolve, and become more.

Writing Tools

As a blacksmith needs a forge, anvil, hammer, and many other instruments I'm unfamiliar with, so must a writer have tools. Luckily, you need very few. If you've found your happy spot with long-hand writing—pen and paper—or a typewriter, stick with it. Otherwise, you need a computer.

Many folks use Microsoft Word or Google Docs. If this works for you, great. For those of you who struggle, there are many novel-writing software to choose from: Novlr, Scrivener, WriteItNow, FocusWriter, and too many to list. Don't forget about the editing tools like AutoCrit,

Grammarly, ProWritingAid, Hemingway Editor, and countless others. I'm not advocating for you to buy one or subscribe, especially if it's not for you, but there are options.

Remember: these are software programs and not a human editor, and they should never replace one. Your editor will thank you if you do, but they'll still find errors. Trust me.

One writer I know enjoys Scrivener and the back-up to the cloud function. He can write on his laptop, then while standing in line at the store, type on his phone. It all syncs up. I use WriteItNow; it doesn't have a cloud upload, and I prefer this method. Depending on your lifestyle, IT-security concerns, and device, you can choose which is best for you.

> **Storytime**: Once, many years ago, I almost quit writing. I was using Word for my novels, but writing is so much more than jotting down sentences in a document. You need to make detailed notes on your book, locations, items, and the like, create characters, event boards, and other useful tools along the way. By this point, you'll amass dozens of documents you've got to save in a file on your desktop. It's not just about the endless scrolling to find a segment in the middle of your book where that one character said or did something, and you've got to reference the moment for a callback.

Many years into my hobby, this was me, but across many different stories. I swam in a sea of endless documents and infinite scrolling. Plus, the stark white screen wasn't helping, not to mention all those red and blue squiggly lines. So, I did a little research. Surely, there had to be something for writers. I found dirt-cheap and expensive platforms alike, from buying outright to subscription-based. I cross-referenced each one to see what they offered as a total product and began selecting my top five. What I ended up with was WriteItNow.

This saved me and my passion for crafting stories.

If writing is a hobby for you, stick with what works and what's free. If you are serious about being a novelist and want to take your long-term career or hobby to the next level, I recommend investing in yourself. You can never go wrong investing in yourself—in all walks of life. You are your greatest commodity. I paid the one-time fee for the software and never regretted it a day in my life. Plus, when they come out with a newer version, you can upgrade at a discounted price.

With WriteItNow, I was able to save all my notes in different little entries under my 'Notes' segment. Characters have their own section where you can free-write—a place where you can type like any other word processor—their description or use the software's aides to help craft one.

There's a name generator, and a tool to help you craft a personality from Myers-Briggs, archetypes, or enneagrams. You can create histories and tether your characters by family relations, interpersonal relationships, or write in whatever you wish. By the end, you can see a chart of how everyone is connected. There are other exciting segments like storyboards, chapter summary details, and more. Some features I use, and some I don't.

By buying WriteItNow, I could take dozens of documents and save them all in one location, and access them with the click of a button. For the first time in years, I was ecstatic and could focus, not wasting my time searching through endless files.

Don't take my word as the only one speaking the gospel. If you are part of a critique group, ask your fellow participants. Do your research and due diligence. What are they using? What other tools can help you? Which one fits your lifestyle and budget? If you want to try WriteItNow, you can download a free demo on their website. What do you have to lose?

In the end, software is just that: software. It won't write your novel for you. It's not perfect in terms of spelling, tenses, grammar, punctuation, or any other issue that might arise. It can aid you, but nothing is infallible.

Chapter 2: Self-Preparation

Overview

In this chapter, we'll tackle what you can do to prepare yourself. Some of these are from research, some self-discovery. You may possess some of these tools in your arsenal already but don't realize it. This book is meant to give you many elements for your tool belt, and hopefully, you'll feel like Batman, ready to take on your fantasy world.

The first and quite crucial element should be obvious: you can't focus with distractions. This means interruptions from people, calls, social media, the construction worker with a jackhammer outside, and yes, I've dealt with that. Every writer I've ever known cannot sit down and begin writing right away. If you can, I envy you. It takes time to find the rhythm and flow. At times, this is slow in coming, and you'll struggle with three hundred words. Yet, on other occasions, you can sit down and knock out a couple thousand words.

The point—don't get up from your desk and limit distractions. Find your seam as quick as possible, and attack hard.

Turn the ringer off on your phone or the notifications. Leave it in another room. You don't need your phone to write. Let me say that again: you don't need your phone to write. These days, it seems we're born with one in our hands. Every minute spent scrolling on social media is a minute you could've written the most significant scene of your career. You must choose which is more important: strangers on the internet or following your passion.

You'll also need to make other hard choices. Do you want to sit and binge-watch a show, go out to a movie, relax and play video games all day? For me, for a while, painting took over. All writing fell to the wayside. I eventually had to stop painting for months to get back on track. Don't let distractions derail you. That said, don't forget to live. Use balance and moderation, but keep your end goal in mind, whatever it may be.

Once you've managed to find time for yourself, don't stop. If you are in the middle of a scene, especially a tense one or action-driven, don't break your rhythm. Nothing can kill your momentum quicker than an interruption. Put a sign on your door, talk with your spouse or significant other, or schedule alone time.

For many years, on my off days, I'd wake up and write from 4:00 a.m. until 6:15 a.m. My drop-dead time was 6:30 a.m., and no matter if I was done with the scene or chapter or not, the daily events of life took over, and I got up from my desk. This is part of the sacrifice I referred to. I sacrificed late nights and rising early to achieve my goals.

I also once had a job where every three months, we'd flop between day shift and night shift. I wrote quite a few stories during the quietest hours. Sometimes, because nothing was going on, I could write about nine hours of my twelve-hour shift. Find what works for you, and stick with it.

What did Thanos say? "The hardest choices require the strongest wills."

A Writer's Strength: Knowing Your Type

Writers come in a plethora of options, like cars. You've got sports cars, sedans, vans, and SUVs. Well, with writing, there's no one way. In fact, you might be a bit of several types. In my earliest days, I was 100% a pantser. A pantser or seat-of-your-pants writer is a type of novelist who sits down and starts the story. There's no outline, but there's an endpoint they want to reach. A notorious pantser is George R.R. Martin, author of *A Song of Ice and Fire*. For those of you who may not make the connection, that's the *Game of Thrones* novels. However, he uses the term Gardner. We'll tackle that in a minute.

There are four types of writers we will be discussing: Pantsers/ Gardners, Outliners/Architects, Edit-as-You-Go, and Snowflakers/ Snowflake method, or, what I like to call, shotgun. As a writer, you need to understand what type you are. Where are your strengths? Let's find out! The beauty of the categories is you can be more of one and less of another, but you can be a combination.

The Pantsers/Gardners style was my main strength for many years. It still is the backbone of my work. This arrangement allows you to sit down and start, and as you type, the ideas flow through your fingertips. More often than not, this choice is linear.

Pros:

Many of my plot twists come from this approach. I may plan one or two, but 90% come from this ritual alone and take me by surprise. If it pulls a fast one on me, the reader will crumble beneath the shock when they read it. What's more, this can drastically alter the outcome of your novel or character arcs, and it's a great way to bring a fresh novelty to storytelling. This process allows for spontaneity not found in the Outliner plan. This book for, the most part, is written using the seat-of-your-pants technique.

Cons:

But there are drawbacks, too. In the post-writing phase, there's a lot of revision and tightening of the bolts of the story. Without an outline to keep you on course, you might go off track. Substantial rewrites may be in your future.

Snowflaking is the second technique, and despite the tongue-in-cheek humor, it's not a bad thing. Like a shotgun blast that scatters everywhere, this writer does the same. This type sits down and says, "I want to write the finale, not the beginning," and immediately jumps to the ending. Then, they want to sink into a juicy segment towards the middle, so they'll do that. This routine continues until the novel is written.

I've used this process before in select moments, but with infrequent use. Sometimes, I find myself wanting to explore a tantalizing scene, or another segment pops in my head and wasn't part of the plan. I'll do whatever I need to. Like those who go to the gym, listen to your mind and body, it will tell you when you need a break, when you feel most refreshed, or what muscles to work.

Pros:

You can tackle whatever you want when you want. Whatever is drawing you, that's what you do. Snowflaking can also go well with outlining. You know where your novel is going, but maybe you want to craft it in a different manner.

Cons:

The downfall of snowflaking is trying to find the thread weaving the tapestry together. Snowflaking also doesn't account for the unexpected. For example, if a personality comes to life and you find yourself drawn to them and want to explore them more, you're in trouble. By the time you realize this, who knows how far into the story you are. Trampling over the same ground again becomes a necessity.

Outliners/Architects are the learn-by-rote tactic used in high school for those who grew up in the '90s or earlier. This manner is terrible … for me. Other novelists and writers fall back on this procedure as time-tested dogma. If that works for you, fantastic, but it's not for everyone, which is okay, too!

Pros:

Charting your course is ideal for mammoth stories and their moving parts, or for a series. In this setting, you can stay on course and not stray far from your narrative. In many ways, your novel can almost write itself by the time you get around to diving deep. Famous authors who outline are Brandon Sanderson and J.K. Rowling.

Cons:
The drawback of outlining everything is the finite space of wiggle room for the unexpected. Maybe you planned for this character to be a secondary or a one-off, and they try to take over the story. Outlining doesn't allow for this, especially if you are dedicated to your path.

Edit-as-you-go means different things to people. You can edit each sentence, paragraph, page, or chapter before moving on, but you won't move on until you are done.

Pros:
You will have little at the end to fix because you've done it along the way. That said, many find this approach the best for them, and if so, they should continue.

Cons:
This method takes a lot of time and can feel like you're treading water. This can be detrimental to your creative health while writing. Editing and creative thinking are too diverse to be beneficial together, and going back to edit takes you out of the flow of the moment. Further, always editing before moving on may drain some of the creative juice your side characters might pick up.

My Style: I'm about 85% pantser, 10% shotgun, and about 5% outlining. I may dabble with editing a line because I'm not in the flow or couldn't ignore the atrocious prose. All that said, my way still varies further. Though I work linearly, I write only characters in such a manner and not the story itself.

At the beginning of a book, I select a member from my cast and stick with them. I don't write anyone else. Let's say I am penning a book of characters that never interact with anyone else except character A. Individuals B-F all meet A, but not each other. I'll commit to character A from start to finish, then pick any of the other ones from start to finish. Each is linear.

This helps me stay in the mindset of one and gives each their distinct voices. If I grow bored with them, it's a sign to me that the reader may also become bored, and I scrutinize where I went wrong. George R.R. Martin also writes his characters this way, something I recently learned. And here I thought I was unique!

If you've found your strength, stick with it. For those uncertain, try each process above until you find the path that sets you free.

Remember: advice is marvelous, but if it doesn't help you, it *can* help others. As Yoda once said, "Pass on what you have learned."

Setting the Mood

Some writers need snacks beside them; others, a beverage. For me, I need coffee when I first start, because I write early in the mornings. This only prepares me to write, but I still need a mood. This is where the backbone of my writing comes into play. I set the mood with music.

As a musician, music is a powerful tool for me. I find that melodies and symphonies move me in ways I cannot adequately express. When going to a theater, I enjoy all aspects, but music resonates with me during the film and long after. A score can make a mediocre movie phenomenal, and only specific composers stir me. No two are alike, and if they are, they need to be more original.

When choosing music, I pick scores from movies that had a profound impact on me. If you find a composer you like, do research. Maybe they made more scores, and you're unaware of their contributions. A valuable tool is the Internet Movie Database or IMDB.com. My all-time favorite is Hans Zimmer.

But not all music will help you in your current scene, and you need to be mindful of how it makes you feel. As a guitarist and drummer, I can't listen to my usual bands unless at the gym. Rock and metal are great music to help you find your pump, but with writing, I will focus on the guitar riffs, insane drum fills, and the lyrics will throw me off. So, I focus on musical scores from movies that I really enjoyed.

I break my music down to playlists and label them. Each starts with the title "Book-" followed by a tag, so they are clumped together. If I need an action scene, I play "Book-Fights." Maybe I want to write an inspirational hero moment, I've got that, too. I even make playlists for specific characters so I can immediately get in the correct "mood." Each scene or chapter I write I switch the playlist as needed.

What about those dark, heartbreaking moments? In movies, the acting moves you, but the ballad sweeping over the scene makes your soul weep. Use the same tactic when writing. If you don't know what kind of mood you need to be in, pick your absolute top-ten favorites and clump them in a playlist and label it "Book-Mood Setting." One song that comes to mind is called *The Dark Knight*, a sixteen-minute ensemble of melodies. Let the music sweep you off your feet and let your imagination soar.

Speaking of *The Dark Knight*, my all-time favorite composer is Hans Zimmer. All his music sounds quite different despite some tell-tale signs that he's the composer. He's got many scores under his belt, and you've heard them: *Pirates of the Caribbean, The Last Samurai, Gladiator, The Da Vinci Code, The Dark Knight* trilogy, *Man of Steel, Interstellar, Inception*, and many more.

When I first started using this method many years ago, I would always know what part of which movie the music accompanied. I still do, but it's in the back of my mind. Now, it's just the music, but the instruments elicit moods.

Have you tried this? If so, does it work for you? If you haven't, give it a go.

Below is a shortlist of some of the composers I use:

Atticus Ross: *The Book of Eli*
Junkie XL: *Mad Max: Fury Road*
James Horner: *Braveheart*
John Paesano: Netflix and Marvel's *Daredevil*
John Williams: *Star Wars*
Michael Giacchino: *Star Trek* and *Rogue One*
Nicholas Hooper: *Harry Potter and the Half-Blood Prince*
Ramin Djawadi: *Game of Thrones*
Rupert Gregson-Williams: *Wonder Woman*
Tom Tykwer, Johnny Klimek, and Reinhold Heil: *Cloud Atlas*
Hildur Guðnadóttir: *Joker*

Do you have any favorite composers? What melodies would go with your book? Give it a try. It might change your writing game.

Target Audience Mentality

I categorize target audience selection—the people you want to read your work—within the self-preparation phase. Yes, it can go in another segment on writing, but this isn't just for your reader but also for you. Selecting a target audience comes with a mindset. It will change your prose, theme and content, and it'll mold you as a writer.

I dare say you can write almost any story for any age bracket, but much will be left by the wayside. There's a reason why *Game of Thrones* is an adult fantasy book instead of a children's book with pictures. When choosing your clientele, you need to know what they expect, not only for the age bracket but content.

I will be the first to admit I don't read much out of my zone, but I have my reasons. I've typically found epic, high fantasy for adults has the hardest learning curve not only in elements of the story but prose and vocabulary. If your first novel is a dive into an adult, epic fantasy, I'd suggest doing your research. If you come with the wrong tone, you'll find many things feeling off about your novel. How different would *The Hunger Games* be written with a Shakespeare delivery? What if *Star Wars* was written with an adolescent's mentality and tone? We'll talk more on tone later.

Bottom line: Target audience and genre should be a focal point of how you prepare yourself. If you're eighteen, and your main character (MC) is an ancient wizard, he wouldn't speak, react, or comport himself like you. We'll dive further into this during character building. This mentality of selecting your targeted range of readers should be established early on.

Some authors write for a broad market, and they're successful, but their appeal comes from a great story with fleshed-out characters minus the gritty reality of adults who are usually the protagonists in the stories. In a book, you're the creator, and things simply don't exist if you don't include them. Your readers are smart, and just because you don't write about something specific, doesn't mean it won't happen off-screen.

It's also important to remember how niche your book might be. Will it appeal to the masses or a specific group and age range? These are essential questions to ask yourself in the preparation phase. Also, your plot's complexity might bump you up or down in your bracket—not to mention how old your characters are.

Speaking of niche audiences, there are things for you to consider and remember. The more specific the elements of your story, i.e., moving further away from a general market, the smaller your reading circle will be. The novel's appeal will influence the readability of your book.

Which do you think is more likely to ensnare numerous readers? A book about raising zombies and talking with them, or a book about zombies where the MC has a hankering for necrophilia? One is going to be much more widely accepted than the other. So, the more specific, the smaller the pool.

My next point: know the difference between themes and preaching. While this isn't something to specifically consider unless needed, you should take a moment to ponder. Like getting into a niche audience with the aforementioned scenario, crafting a story with themes can be divisive or alienating, so proceed with care. There's a stark difference between writing a book that happens to have a theme, and using your book as a vehicle to preach (on any topic). If you find yourself in the latter, don't be surprised when folks put down your book. Preaching real-world issues through a book (or established franchises in movies) can put your readers off. Again, you're restricting the readability and target pool.

This brings me to the last point of this little segment. Reading fiction is about escapism—which is why we're not reading self-help or nonfiction. People enjoy movies about superheroes, play games about distant places among the stars, or read journeys through Middle Earth. We want to be swept away by a great story with excellent characters, not fall face-first into a book with real-world issues slapping us every few pages.

What do I mean by real-world problems? If you turn on the TV, or dig through any considerable concern in the last twenty years and then write about it specifically to get your belief (as the author) across, that'd be construed as such. Again, there's a difference in a theme and preaching.

So, what are you writing? A children's book? Something for teens? Or is the subject matter, themes, and elements more suited for adults? Do a little soul searching, nail it down, and get ready for building your world and story.

Chapter 3: Preparing for the Story: Setting Structure

Simplistic Approach

At the risk of being crucified by other writers, dare I say, in terms of storytelling, you need three things: the inciting incident, the critical choice, and the climax.

Yes, this is a gross oversimplification. There's more to building a story structure, but all three are in each of the other crafting methods. Consider these must-hit staples.

What I'm trying to say is, if you find something that works for you, as long as you have those three elements, go for it. In the end, if you fail, well, at least you tried, but if you succeed, we may all be hailing you as the next writing genius. Let's move on.

Story Structure

It goes without saying, but your story needs propulsion. Something needs to be happening for the reader to experience progress. If nothing transpires, the narrative becomes stale, and the reader treads water. This is where they become bored and put the book down.

You don't need high-octane explosions to feel a pace or progression, but I'm sure, in some cases, it helps. *Transformers* anyone? Okay, bad example.

Remember: action doesn't only mean car chases, shootouts, or fistfights. Let's take a quick peek at *Star Wars* (SW) and *The Empire Strikes Back* (ESB). In *SW*, the story is propelled by the need to get the Death Star plans to Senator Bail Organa of Alderaan. Princess Leia does this by enlisting R2 to seek out General Kenobi. Streamlining all the setbacks, they board the Falcon and head to Alderaan, sneak aboard the Death Star, knock out the tractor beam, rescue the princess and escape, but not without a cost. And by now, you should know the rest of the story.

The point I'm making is this series of events snowballs. *SW* is the classical Hero's Journey, which we'll discuss later.

Now, let's shift to *ESB*, a different kind of movie. In many ways, it's an inverse of *SW*. In *SW*, the big battle is at the end, the Empire vs. the Rebellion. In *ESB*, the stereotypical 'climactic' battle is at the beginning. Then, instead of the group coming together to set to a task, they split up and go their separate ways.

In this movie, we go deeper into the characters than what we first learned in *SW*, especially Luke. He goes off to train with Yoda. As a child, I liked Yoda because he was cool and funny, yet powerful and wise. I was awed he could lift an X-wing. At an early age, I knew the story lagged in this section—at least as a kid, I did. Why?

Because the pacing slowed despite the depth of character building going on. There weren't flashy lasers, ships, and lightsabers—the things kids really care about. In a story, going deeper into a character *can* mean the pace slows, but it doesn't mean stopping all progression. Every time we check in on Luke at Dagobah, he's learning more, and we see headway.

To offset this slower momentum, we often jump to Vader or Han and Leia with them running from the Empire. This is where the tempo picks back up as they dodge TIE fighters, Star Destroyers, and asteroids. There's action, which gives the appearance of pace, if not advancement, which is better than a slow space chase. Further, there's another shadowy figure to contend with: Boba Fett.

When writing a story, you need a mix of action/pace and character progression and to discover a perfect balance. I've often found when writing—and reading other people's stories—the more introspective you go in a character's head, the slower the tempo becomes for the reader and story. You must augment this with some form of action, or at the least, progress.

This brings up many ways to craft a story, whether the Three Act Structure, Harmon's Circle, LOCK Structure, Hero's Journey, or Four Corner Opposition. You can combine some of these elements to create a blended story method. The Three Act or the Four Corners will go well with the Hero's Journey or Harmon's Circle. If you're confused by what I'm talking about, don't worry, it's covered later in this chapter.

In all honesty, there are so many structures available—it'd take too long to write, but these are the prominent ones. I've found, however, simplicity is critical when structuring. That's not to say your novel needs to be simple, or your twists and turns can't be complicated. As the saying goes, don't try to reinvent the wheel, but not all wheels are molded the same.

How I Plot a Story

Most folks, when it comes to a story idea, think of the overall plot first. This is where I differ. Yes, the idea or notion of the story comes to me, but I don't dwell on it. Instead, I pivot and think of characters, both what I want and what the story needs. I typically write a character-driven story rather than plot-driven. Since I'm not the norm, we'll cover plotting first.

In my first book, *The Bearer of Secrets*, I'm often asked, "How do you plot a story that complex?" The simple answer? I don't. However, as I write more, I do what I call glance-back plotting. If a character said something cryptic or interesting, or referenced some person, place, or thing, I draw that out as the base of future plotlines. But, I'm getting ahead of myself.

As a pantser, I sit down and write. Very little time or energy is spent on plotting. Only in certain circumstances do I figure specific segments before writing them. Ideas come to me, and I incorporate them as needed. If I can't use a particular plan, I file it away for later. Sometimes, I'll write down one or two sentences on what I need to accomplish as a focal point, so I don't forget.

That's not to say I don't have an idea where I'm going. There's an end goal in mind and tent poles, big staples in the story to hit, but otherwise, the journey to those markers isn't plotted. It's as much an adventure for me as for the character and reader.

My first book, *The Bearer of Secrets*, did come to me in a dream, so I had a template in which to work. Fleshing out the sequel also came easy. I saw the start of their stories, and I progressed them to their final destination, but with added twists. New folks introduced in the sequel turned plotlines on its head at one point or another. When figuring out the sequel, I narrow the base down to a single sentence or question: where does my cast *need* to go from here? Most of the time, I look at this in three ways:

1. What is the most logical outcome?
2. What would I or my characters like to see happen?
3. How can I turn this on its head, go into left field, and still deliver a believable and fascinating story?

From here, I find a solution that's a mix of all three. A strict personal rule helps me: Never do a happy ending. Everyone wants a happy ending in real life, to be swept away by characters and story. When you read a character who suffers, our lives don't seem so bad. This is what I try to deliver in a story, something fantastical and unique with great depth and a profound impact.

I've also been asked, "Well, how do you know what your story needs if you don't plot?" That answer comes a little simpler and with more substance: Characters. I flesh out my characters, which we'll be covering later, and their personalities and choices change my story. I don't direct them where to go, they tell me what they need. In essence, I look at my

25

characters as real people, and you want them to come across as such, but that's for the character chapter.

Let's take *Star Wars: A New Hope*, and assume this is your story. Use the question I posed earlier: Where does my cast *need* to go from here? Following the character R2-D2, he has one clear goal: Find Obi-Wan Kenobi and deliver the Death Star plans. That's where he *needs* to go.

1. What is the most logical outcome? He finds Obi-Wan or gets captured by Darth Vader's stormtroopers.

2. What would I or my characters like to see happen? R2 finds Obi-Wan and brings Luke into the story.

3. How can I turn this on its head, go left field, and still deliver a believable and fascinating story?

R2 sets out at night to find Obi-Wan. Leaving Luke and C-3PO behind, R2 makes his way to Mos Eisley Spaceport. He doesn't know where Kenobi lives, and Tatooine's a backwater planet without the internet, so he'll go to the nearest city and hope for a directory there. Upon arrival, he's captured by a pirate gang who slap a restraining bolt on him and force him into service aboard their ship. They leave the spaceport and set a destination for deeper space.

Now, he's got a series of goals: removing the restraining bolt, figuring out where he is, escaping the gang, returning to Tatooine, and finding Kenobi.

Your other characters' storylines have changed now. Will Luke take off after him, go to Tosche Station to pick up power converters, or stay on the moisture farm? Now, let's say I go with the third option and R2 is captured.

This fulfills the second question: bring Luke into the story. Uncle Owen tells Luke to track down their droid. Now, he's in the story. With this tale unfolding the way it's going, it no longer has a logical outcome, the response to the first question. Anything can happen.

Following this thread, the pirates set a course for deep space, but they're captured by Darth Vader's Star Destroyer. Now, the Death Star plans come full circle and back into the hands of the enemy, but they are unaware. The pirates are dealt with, and R2 is now in the service of the Empire. Luke's coming after him and is also captured.

In a single setting, we now have R2, the plans, Vader, and now Luke. Luke's brought before Darth Vader, and the Sith Lord senses the potential of the Force within him. Vader could discover that Luke is his son, or Vader takes him as an apprentice to overthrow the Emperor, or Vader kills him outright as a threat to his power.

How different would the *Star Wars* saga be if this happened?

Let's say Vader turns Luke to the dark side. The Rebellion's only hope is Princess Leia, but she's captured. How will she be freed now? Will Obi-Wan sense a disturbance in the Force?

Here's where answering these questions gets tricky. You've got to remember R2 isn't your main protagonist—unless he is—and his arc weaves with other plotlines. If R2 is a side character, make sure your answers and directions fit your overall narrative. This can either be done on the front end by outlining, fixed during, or after the first draft. Ninety-five percent of the time, I wait until after the first draft unless something is easily fixed.

Now, let's move on to some other methods of plotting.

The 5 W's

Every book starts with a single idea. You may have met people who say, "I've got a great idea for a book!" And you say, "Tell me about it." Then, they enter a fifteen-minute discourse of jumbled thoughts and convoluted, paper-thin characters.

But that's expected.

I call this the rough draft of thoughts. Much like your manuscript's rough draft, so too must you have a rough idea of what it will be about. But how do we make the fifteen-minute exposition into something worthy of writing? We simplify.

My ideology ties directly into the one-sentence summary after the novel is written. The back jacket blurb talks about what the book entails, but first, you must sell your book to an agent or publisher, or for an ad if you self-publish. This is much harder than it sounds.

Writing is sometimes difficult, but in the confines of a maximum word count of about fifteen to eighteen is grueling. These limits may vary from less to more and depend on need and structure. How do you summarize your finished product into a sentence?

In many ways, the beginning notions of a book and the summary of the finished product are congruent. When building your story, strip out everything to the core elements.

What is your tale about? A revenge novel? A crime mystery? A coming-of-age narrative? A sci-fi thriller?

In many ways, it's almost like picking your genre, and though your genre may be sci-fi, it could still be a crime mystery. A coming-of-age revenge story could be set in a fantasy world.

To expand both on the beginning notion and the final one-line synopsis, I utilize the five W's—five dubs—who, what, when, where, and why. In both, we want simplicity while revealing why this book/idea is good to pursue.

In this case, I'd limit the characters to two unless set in an established world. If we expected the imminent arrival of a *Star Wars* novel, I would assume the sentence and the blurb to talk about Han, Luke, and Leia. Use discretion but simplify. Also, don't try to cram every subplot, just the main point.

Five W's
Who: MC, protagonist, villain …
What: What is going on? What's the conflict or choice to be made?
Where: What setting does this take place in? Where are we going?
When: Is time a factor?
Why: (if applicable)

For those utilizing this for crafting a story, don't worry about character or location names, but write in a manner you will recollect. Let us say you are going to pen *The Lord of the Rings*, but you don't know all the facts. You could start your one-sentence analysis like this: "Little dude seeks to destroy an unknown artifact that holds the soul and power of the villain."

Why is the artifact unknown? Well, we haven't made it a ring yet. Why is he little? I don't know, maybe he is young or of a different race. There aren't many books with gnome-like creatures as leads. Who's the villain, and where does he reside? Somewhere far away … it's going to take a long time … like three books and nine hours of film, but it'll be epic!

Remember: This is a rough idea, the infancy of crafting your story. You don't need all the answers now.

Now, if you wrote *LOTR*, how would you write the one-line encapsulation? Maybe like this: "Frodo must journey to the fiery depths of Mordor to destroy the one ring of power before it claims his soul or falls into the hands of the dark lord." Not perfect, but a start.

Now, practice by trimming down. In this instance, I chose to leave out the 'when' (time frame) but explained why. For a solid one-sentence extract or crafting the first thoughts of your novel, the more W's you can add, the better.

Once you've fleshed out your idea to a single line, let's stretch to two. Craft a little more detail. After two sentences, write a paragraph. Keep utilizing your previous writing as the building blocks for your current work. We are building to craft characters, locations, plot/outline, and possible subplots.

Need more practice? Try summaries for popular movies, anime, or TV shows: *Star Wars, Terminator, Inception* (that one would be tricky!), *The Dark Knight, Fried Green Tomatoes, Attack on Titan, Castle, Lost* ... Stretch yourself and imagine one line at a time.

The 3 Act Structure

When discovering a new idea, many factors are involved: What's the story, and who is the story about? These two elements are the driving points of building a plotline. I'm not advocating that you can't create a storyline without knowing who your character is, but it might be easier with an idea of who your character is before nailing down an embarrassing and tragic moment in their past.

Below is the quick view (some things I've added), followed by a broken-down model.

ACT I

1: The Rut: The first chapter, life is going on as usual, preparation for the unexpected.

A: Spark: The change in their lives that starts the story

2: Choice and Quest: The beginning of the journey

A: Aspiration & Purpose

ACT II

B: Setback/ Side Quest

3: Rise to Climax

A: Epiphany

B: Critical Choice: Often a sacrifice.

ACT III

C: Setback 2/Side Quest resolution

4: Climax: All hell breaks loose. Did all the characters come together, or did they remain their own storylines?

5: Resolution and Effects: Though they sound the same, they aren't. With every event, two parts propel it: cause and effect. The cause was the start, and the resolution is the end of the quest, and then the effects occur.

A: Effects: What's going on in the wake of turmoil? What does it look like when the dust settles?

With an idea of the overall structure, let's peer more closely and ask ourselves the tough questions. Before we begin, glance above. Any line starting with a letter can be moved around, tailored to your specific needs. Keep that in mind while crafting your plot. Much of the following goes hand in hand with character creation.

ACT I: The Rut: This is life going on as usual. We are getting an idea of what our character's life was like before the spark. In the *Harry Potter* books, this is the summer portion of the story, the front end. For this segment, concerning character and story purposes, ask yourself the following questions:

What is your main character? Hero? Anti-hero? Villain? Or are they a villain and don't realize it?

Who is your MC? How do they talk, think, act? What is their moral code? What are their beliefs (religion and mores)? What are their strengths/weaknesses? Any unique qualities or powers?

The Spark: This is what changes the story from dull to exciting. Keep in mind, there may be more than one spark. In the movie, *Lord of the Rings: Fellowship of the Ring*, several smaller sparks lead to the quest. The first is Gandalf's arrival in the Shire. This mini-spark segues to another mini-spark, Bilbo's party, to another mini-spark, leaving behind the ring of power, to yet another, Gandalf's discovery of its actual design. Gandalf returns to the Shire and thus begins the story proper.

Quest: You may have an idea of what this entails, but how can you make the temptations more irresistible and the stakes higher? What little twist can you add to make it more substantial? In *The Bourne Identity*, Marie is caught between the shadow organization and their target. To make matters worse, the target, Jason Bourne, doesn't know who he is or why they're after him. This is the twist; otherwise, it's a rehash of *Rambo: First Blood* minus Marie and the memory loss.

Is there a deadline (time pressure) for the action to come to a resolution? Can one be introduced? Who can create it? Does the hero only have until the next full moon? The TV series *24* comes to mind. The whole story takes place within a day. This is the timer.

What are the alternative ideas to handle the situation? Can supporting cast help articulate those ideas or be forceful for the alternative method? In creating a supporting cast around your MC, bringing people with different strengths, weaknesses, ideologies, and backgrounds than your protagonist.

ACT II: Setback and Side Quest: How can we hurt our characters physically, mentally, and emotionally? How can we make them grow and evolve?

What is the best outcome of this evolution? What is the worst? Did they give up their beliefs or reinforce them?

Rise to Climax: We are making headway, but not quite to the end. This should be the bulk of your second act. In *The Empire Strikes Back*, this portion is Luke training with Yoda, preparing him for the climactic battle with Darth Vader at Cloud City. Also, Han and Leia are hiding in the asteroid field, trying to escape the Empire, and to fix the Falcon.

Make sure you touch back on your side quest or setback. Is it resolved, or can it be carried to the climax? Don't forget about it. In this instance, Han and Leia evade the Empire, but the Falcon isn't fixed. Han chooses to go to Cloud City because of Lando, an old friend, but the Falcon isn't repaired.

Epiphany: Think about character development: Do they grow? Do they become worse? No change? One epiphany in *EBS* is Luke having a vision of Han and Leia in pain. Another epiphany is when Darth Vader reveals the truth to Luke. That's the beauty of this method—you can use multiples of something and move them around on the board.

ACT III: Climax: Think about the height. Things are bad, but can we raise the tension? How can we make them worse? It isn't simply stabbing them with a knife—it's the twist, too.

Critical Choice: This is where the hero is resolved to carry out the plan. For *The Empire Strikes Back*, this is when Luke rushes off to Cloud City to confront Vader. In *Harry Potter and the Deathly Hallows*, this is where Harry decides to meet Voldemort in the Forbidden Forest and face his death. *In The Return of the King*, Frodo keeps the ring.

After the climactic battle or situation comes the resolution and effects. The resolution deals with the main cast and MC. Are they a better person? Did they die? Did they revert to their former self? Realistically, people change in small ways, not in grand and sweeping ways most stories show.

One enjoyable part of *Harry Potter* was that while the character grew over the series, he remained faithful to his core elements. After defeating Voldemort, he didn't congratulate himself or let the ego take hold. He returned to his life, what was left, fixed his wand, and his friends survived with him. So, remember: resolution deals with the leads.

Effects: You could clump this with the resolution if that's all the story entails, but it should have a more global aspect. Life goes on, *but nothing's the same*. In *Return of the Jedi*, we don't see the effects until the re-release with the extra scenes added at the end showing other planets. This is part of the effect.

An effect would entail seeing a new government installed, and who leads the new administration. For that story, you'd need to read the *Star Wars Legends (Expanded Universe)* novels, which I highly encourage and endorse. Over a hundred books with great stories spanning thousands of years.

Does this method suit you? If so, use it. Ideas are free, and the three-act structure is only meant to help guide the crafting of your story into a recognizable structure. However, a drawback using this method is the formulaic feel to novels and movies. But not every story uses the three-act. This is primarily used for older stories, think Shakespeare plays, and Hollywood movie scripts.

Again, not all movies follow the three-act structure. A good example of this is *Batman Begins* and *The Dark Knight*. Some argue the Three Act Structure is obsolete, and I tend to agree, but you decide for you and what helps your story.

Let's move on to another method.

The LOCK Structure

LOCK is straightforward compared to the ones you've read so far. The beauty is that you can use this for the book, chapter, scene, etc. You can scale as needed. See LOCK below:

Lead
Objective
Confrontation
Knockout

Lead: Your lead character needs to be a visceral creature, filled with flaws, weaknesses, desires, and dreams. Make them compelling, and they'll carry your story, and your reader will want to follow them more.

Objective: The objectives of your lead should be laid out. Objectives should be goals, both personal and external—what the story needs. You can list these one at a time—if you're outlining—or you can clump them together. You can repeat the LOCK pattern as much as necessary. Objectives create a driving force in the narration, friction with internal and external conflict. There are many goals within your book—personal, external, the sidekick's, the mentor's, the bad guy, etc.

Confrontation: This conflict is derived from your lead going about their objective and coming against opposing forces. While they may want to achieve the same end goals, their methods for reaching them diverge. This is one of many conflicts you can discover. Also, confrontation may not necessarily be against something you can see or fight against; it could be a story of Man vs. Nature.

Knockout: is used in place of the climax, a satisfactory resolution.

Again, this method can be used to break down scenes, chapters, act, or the story as the whole. Try this on a movie you love. Can you spot the telling elements within? Practice this with other films, and pretty soon, you won't be able to shut it out. Writing is both a blessing and a curse.

The Yes, but/No, and Plot

This is another method I've heard about over the years but never incorporated. Theoretically, because of its simplicity, you could use it for world-building and plot. It's a simple series of answers you use at the start of your explanation as you meander through your story, propelling your narrative by forcing you to finish the sentence.

Example:

Does Luke Skywalker learn the secret message R2-D2 carries within him?

Yes, but only after he chases him down in the desert and meets old Ben Kenobi.

Is Luke going to do anything?

No, and he tries to leave before it gets too late. He'll be in trouble with Uncle Owen. He offers Kenobi a ride to Mos Eisley spaceport.

You can use this throughout your entire plotting process. The versatility of this method is limited by the beginning portion of the answer and can become repetitive.

For the world-building portion in a fantasy world—or any setting—you can use it when crafting races.

Example:

Are dwarves in your book?

Yes, but they're different. They have hardened shells on the domes of their heads and often use that to attack during fights.

Do these dwarves have bushy beards?

No, and they don't have hair underneath the domes on their heads. They look like little, hairless moles.

Since this method is fairly straightforward, let's move on to more complex elements.

Monomyth: The Hero's Journey

The hero's journey is the staple of movies and novels for generations. We see it more than you realize—unless you know what you're looking for. Without intending to sound paradoxical, this is the simultaneously familiar and foreign to me in terms of story structure. I understand what it is, I recognize elements, but I don't, with forethought in mind, use the hero's journey. Does my story have these elements in them? For the most part, but they're never designed to mirror since I'm a pantser. Let's dive in.

The most notorious movie I can think of is *Star Wars (SW)*, and the best example of a movie adaptation from a book is *The Lord of the Rings (LOTR)*. Whether you're a die-hard Tolkien fan and love the books but hate the movies, this is an excellent example of the hero's journey, if you examine the trilogy as a whole.

So, what is the monomyth? It's a circular diagram with points along the way. Some say this is eight points, twelve, or seventeen, depending on who you ask. The most prominent one I've seen is the seventeen point. Some combine elements to make a smaller circle. It depends on your preference.

The circle is divided, horizontally, to reference the known vs. unknown. This line is in the upper one-third of the circle, as most stories take place in unknown elements. Others break the circle down into pie-shaped wedges: the departure, initiation, and the return. To illustrate this, I'll be using a blend of *SW* and *LOTR* trilogy—the reason for the trilogy is because one movie doesn't encompass the entire hero's journey.

Here we go:

The Known/Ordinary World—The top one-third. In the Three Act Structure, this is Act One.

1: Call to Adventure—Luke Skywalker hears the call to adventure when he discovers the hidden message from Princess Leia. "Help me, Obi-Wan Kenobi, you're my only hope."

2: Refusal of the Call—Despite whether your MC wants to go on the journey or not, they refuse.

Kenobi to Luke: "You must learn the ways of the Force if you're to come with me to Alderaan."

Luke: "Alderaan? I'm not going to Alderaan. I've got to get home. It's late, I'm in for it as it is."

Kenobi: "I need your help, Luke. She needs your help. I'm getting too old for this sort of thing."

Luke: "I can't get involved. I've got work to do. It's not that I like the Empire, I hate it, but there's nothing I can do about it right now."

3: Meeting the Mentor/Crossing the Threshold—In *SW*, Luke's already met his mentor by now, Kenobi, so crossing the threshold fits. This threshold is when Luke learns the Empire is hunting the droids, which can lead them back to the farm. He rushes off to warn his uncle and aunt, only to find them dead.

Luke to Kenobi: "There's nothing for me here, now. I want to come with you, learn the ways of the Force, and become a Jedi like my father."

Into the Unknown—The bottom two-thirds. Begin Act Two.

This next segment is comprised—again, depending on who you ask —with multiple points. To simplify, I will follow the structure of *SW*, but I will list all the points. In the bottom two-thirds, you have: The Belly of the Whale, The Road of Trials, Meeting with the Goddess, Temptress from the Path, Atonement, The Ultimate Low, The Ultimate Boon/ Transformation, and the Refusal of the Return.

Now, back to *SW*.

4: The Belly of the Whale and Road to Trials—Luke and Kenobi meet Han and Chewbacca, hire them for passage to Alderaan, escape the stormtroopers and Star Destroyers above Tatooine, and Luke begins training in the Force. As part of the final portion of Road to Trials, they must sneak aboard the Death Star.

Side Note: In this segment, finding the Death Star—which is not their plan—is a side quest or set back in the Three Act Structure.

5: Meeting the Goddess—In this instance, it's Luke finding and rescuing Princess Leia. I wouldn't say rescue her, as she holds her own once released, but she did need someone to open the door. And that's why we all love Leia.

6: The Ultimate Low—While escaping, Luke sees Darth Vader kill Kenobi in a lightsaber duel. At this point, Luke has lost everything.

7: The Ultimate Boon—Whether he realizes it or not, Luke now has the ultimate boon, though he discovered it earlier. Kenobi can still guide him through the Force. When Luke is shooting the stormtroopers, Kenobi urges him, "Run, Luke, run." This ultimate boon will help him later destroy the Death Star.

8: The Magic Flight—This can take many shapes depending on the need and the story. The mission still looms ahead of Luke. He released the princess and still has the Death Star plans. Now, it's time to flee. They take off in the Falcon and destroy the pursuing TIE fighters.

Begin Act III.

9: Refusal of the Return/Transformation: Instead of giving up, Luke continues, completes the mission, joins the Rebellion, and leaves to fight the Death Star.

10: Rescue from Without—The battle above Yavin isn't going well for the Rebellion, but Luke is closing in on his target. Two crucial points happen here, the ultimate boon makes a resurgence in the form of Kenobi telling Luke to, "Let go," and Han Solo returns to save Luke from Vader during the trench run.

11: Master of Two Worlds—Luke lets the torpedoes fly, and they go down the exhaust port. The remaining pilots retreat, and the Death Star is blown up. In the background, Kenobi says, "Remember Luke, the Force will be with you always." Luke returns to the rebel base.

12: The Return/Freedom to Live—The story closes out with the medal ceremony—symbolizing the freedom to live—but it isn't a true hero's journey, as the hero returns home a changed person.

This is where we shift to *LOTR*. At the end of the third film, Frodo and the hobbits return to the Shire, and we can visually tell how much they've changed, contrasted with the merriment around them. They seem world-savvy with a hollowness to their eyes, as if the pleasures of the Shire aren't enough anymore. The stark distinction I want to make is between Sam and Frodo.

Sam now dares to ask Rosie to marry him. After facing goblins and the fires of Mt. Doom, this is paltry. Frodo, on the other hand, has a sense of loss, and yes, part of that is innocence, but also a loss of purpose.

Whatever the novels or movie intends, look at it in this light: Sam comes back as a better person. Frodo comes back, changed—and not for the better—and can no longer stay in the Shire. You could say this is another call to adventure.

These two outcomes are usually the endings of stories. Are there any other kinds of conclusions to the hero's journey? I challenge you to find or make a different ending.

Harmon's Circle

Harmon's Circle is a rendition of the Monomyth in the previous section but simplified. I actually enjoy Harmon's Circle more, and if I'm ever stuck in the future, I'll be using this method. What's beautiful about this version is that it can be used for a book, act, segment, chapter, or scene. Not only that, but you can also make it match what you need—an emotional reaction from your characters, dialogue, whatever you wish, all you have to do is change a few words around.

Let's begin:

1: A character is in their zone of comfort.

2: But they want/need something.

3: They enter an unfamiliar situation, the start of your journey.

4: They adapt to the new environment.

5: They get what they wanted, or do they?

6: They pay a heavy price.

7: They return to their familiar situation.

8: But they've changed.

But there's an even shorter one.

1: You—The Protagonist

2: Need—Something isn't right, external vs. internal need

3: Go—Crossing the Threshold.

Enter the Chaos Realm.

4: Search—The Road of Trials.

5: Find—Meeting the Goddess.

6: Pay—Paying the price

Emerge from Chaos Realm

7: Return—Homeward Bound

8: Change—Master of both worlds. Often a visual change. The hero is different.

As you can see, the simplicity of Harmon's Circle can make extrapolating ideas quicker and easier. Since we spent a lot of time on the Monomyth, and Harmon's Circle is an abridged version, we'll move on. But I will say, the questions the circle presents, you should be asking your characters always. They will guide you in the story, at least, that's how I view a narration. Some successful authors find the other way easier: building a tale and then molding the players to it. There's no right and wrong way to write. Find your way.

Chapter 4: Building Your World

Losing Focus

Many people get lost in world-building. They think this is the end-all, be-all. As a writer, you've got to keep perspective. A story isn't about the world, though it is an element of the story. Your novel is a mix of characters, location, and plot. Many writers world-build too much, which delays writing the actual story.

Location plays a significant role in your novel; just look at Hogwarts in *Harry Potter*. While Rowling shows you the uniqueness of the place, and with each subsequent book you learn more, it's only a location. The story is about Harry. You must keep this in mind when writing your manuscript. World-building is excellent, but there's a limit. You need to find that balance.

Why Not Settle for Earth?

Most of the time, in epic fantasy, Earth isn't a factor. In fact, most stories take place on another world altogether. Why? Well, it's a staple. Someone else would argue it's expected. Fantastical worlds are often set on different planets to allow these elements to become part of the story and history. Or, in other words: escapism.

There are several reasons, and all are different for each author. Yet, some writers come out long after their works are circulating to say, "Yes, it's Earth, but ..." the story is so far in the past it might as well be another world, or so far in the future that everything has reset. Without slogging through all their motivations, I'll tackle some of mine.

In my earliest drafts, *The Dark Legacy* series, my story did take place on Earth but in different dimensions. In essence, two people could inhabit the same place at the same time yet not interact because of the different planes of existence. The main villain's goal was to merge the two realms together and wipe out mankind. You'd then have magic users battling jets, ships, Marines, and all our modern technology.

Eventually, I decided this wasn't what I wanted to do. Further, my other ideas clashed with the realism of Earth. My thought process: if you settle a story on Earth, you've got to abide by the rules that govern it.

So, I moved my story elsewhere.

I chose to create the world of Ermaeyth. Here, I had absolute authority to make what I wanted, ignore what I wished, and give my world different constants. Further, I didn't have to worry about explaining how something could exist in a world of humans, evolution, and religions. So, I removed this headache.

As the revisions went on, I also realized how strange it would be to clash epic fantasy with the modern-day world. While a tantalizing notion, I found that my heart wasn't in the idea, so I discarded.

However, I noticed my book was too replete with nods to Earth to be mere coincidence, so I changed the story to account for this. In short: Earth is a world they discovered, and we humans came from Ermaeyth. This is why there are many ties between the worlds, us remembering in some way of our origins. This, to me, was a better idea. Moreover, Earth is never mentioned directly by name, so the impact on the series is minimal.

Other stories had success setting up shop on our world. *Harry Potter* is a prime example of a world within ours. Wizards hide in plain sight, so to speak. I've heard *The Wheel of Time* takes place on Earth, as does *Shannara. Lord of the Rings* is our distant past.

So, where is your story taking place? Are you going to build a new planet, or is your tale going to settle down on Earth? If so, is it a futuristic version that's seen the apocalypse or so far in the past no one can remember? This is your time to flesh all that out.

Questions for an Asinine World

I once talked to an acquaintance of mine in the early years of writing my first novel. I told her about the world, its inhabitants, and little tidbits I thought were interesting, but she disagreed. Being a "picky" reader, she started to rant about what was wrong with my world, asking why I wasn't talking about X, Y, and Z.

At the time, my simple answer was, well, it's not part of my world, so why do I need to add those details?

I went through a slog of inquiries shredding my book, writing, ideas, and motivation. The first time I'd ever opened up to anyone, and she wasn't kind—remember this later in the book. To this day, I've never experienced anything similar.

Maybe it marred me because it was the first, but I vowed never to give someone a reason to do so again. Granted, she posed some decent questions, but seventy-five percent were asinine and not relative to the story. Below is a list of examples, some I recollect, some made up.

"What is the currency exchange rate between the US dollar and your money system? Do they use a sewer in their house? If not, where does it all go? Who deals with that? Where do they take it? What kind of government is yours, a republic, oligarchy, dictatorship, etc.? Where did the nobles get their money? Why do they age at a slower rate? Why doesn't anyone catalog all the magical users in your world? Do they register somewhere? Why don't the lesser magical people rally against the more prevalent magical users? What judicial system do they use? Are there judges and lawyers? What kind of roads do they have? How did they make them?"

You get the idea.

I've only ever read one book that talked about sewage and plumbing, and it was an intrinsic part of creating the world: *To Light A Candle* by Mercedes Lackey and James Mallory. If you've never read it, I highly encourage you to read the trilogy. You want to talk about meticulous world-building? You'll find a level of detail there that I never imagined before.

I digress.

Well, since I don't follow a sewage worker as an expressed POV, I didn't really worry about it. Since it's medieval times or more archaic, they used chamberpots. You don't need a detailed account of the maid or her day while she cleans.

Believe it or not, to this day, this helps me mold my worlds, all those questions she asked. Something positive came from the negativity. I learned what no one is going to ask. Some things will be taken without any explanation. If you detailed every little thing on one street in the city, you'd spend fifty pages, and about forty-nine of those are going to be technicalities your reader doesn't care about. We aren't in the business to bore them.

Over the many years of writing, I've honed my skills, learning rules to live by—which we'll get to later—and found what you already know: set up the scene with the fewest number of words possible while painting a vivid picture. Spare no expense in detail, but sacrifice the lengthy prose on the altar of precision.

Have you ever had someone ask asinine questions about your world? Did they nitpick? Were the queries banal or productive? Even in times like these, you can still learn something.

My World Building Method

Let me declare what I'm about to tell you may not work for you. If you're an outliner, you might want to skim or skip. Since I'm a pantser, all my advice will come from this method. If this works for you, excellent! If not, find your own approach.

When I do world-build a specific element of my story, I drill down to the gritty details, summarize the whole thing, and try to cut ninety percent when I insert. Other things, like how my Krey forge their dragon plate armor, well, more detail is in order.

The story in my head plays out like a movie, a constantly-moving sweep. Unfortunately, the pause button doesn't work. I try to write down everything I see in the first go. In my revisions, I can recall what I initially saw, and flesh the scene out with added details.

Another unwritten rule I generally follow is to not world build until needed. I know you're going to say that's crazy, but hear me out.

One: I don't like wasting time, and writing time is precious. I don't want to world-build something that will never be in the book.

Two: If I think of a concept that I like, I write it down in the most succinct way possible and get back to the story. This way, I won't forget. If it doesn't make the novel, I'll recycle it for later.

Three: building a world takes a lot of time. When I sit and think about my world, trying to fill in every nuanced detail, I feel like I'm spinning my wheels and getting nowhere. I want to always be moving forward.

Four: The first seventy to ninety thousand words are the hardest for me. Once I pass this mark, the opus flies from my fingertips because the world has taken shape, I understand my characters, and I've got a good notion where I'm going. If I stop during this part to world build everything, I'll never finish.

Five: Did I mention it takes time? I've been "world-building" a story in my head for years now. I've never written a word. Sure, I write down the thoughts and stuff, but none of the story has been written. Needless to say, that story is on the back burner and won't see the light of day for years. Further, since I tie all my work together in a shared universe, I need to figure out how they fit.

A notorious author with great worlds is Brandon Sanderson. Many folks remark at how many novels he spits out. And yes, it's true. What I'd love to ask him is how long ago he started the world-building process before he ever wrote a word? I bet some of the answers would be years, too.

Those are the reasons why I don't world build until needed. However, if someone I know is an avid fantasy reader who'd love to talk about my world, I will sit and toss ideas all night. I had about a half-dozen of those with a good friend in Okinawa named Josh. He streamlined months of thinking. Some of his thoughts I incorporated. You can thank him for giving me the initial idea of the Krey by adding bloodlusters into the mix.

Want to deep dive? Josh, the friend above, read an early draft of my novel, and at one point, a character threw down two gold coins for a room at an inn. He came to me and said, "What are you thinking? That's way too much for a room. You need to define your currency." He proceeded to tell me about all the other currencies in the books he read.

This hit home. He was right! I needed to define my money, but where would I start? This is one of those instances where I sat down for world-building and didn't start the novel again until I came up with the solution. I cracked it pretty quickly, within two days.

I started researching how much stuff cost in medieval times, then I converted to cash. But I had to switch that European money into American. Slowly, I started an excel spreadsheet—back before I had writing software—filled with how much armor, swords, horses, wine, a room at an inn, a wedding with a feast, clothes, and shoes cost.

Then I thought, what do I have in my book that can be relative to today? That answer came in the way of the commanding officer in the army I created. I searched how much a four-star general makes per month, backward-convert into ancient funds, and built my legal tender.

Instead of doing something complex, I tried to simplify as much as possible. I ended up with bits, chips, bright eyes, and ingots. Bits, a copper coin, was equal to one dollar, which I called scepters. Thirty scepters/bits/dollars equaled a silver chip. Twenty silver chips, which is six hundred dollars/scepters, equaled one bright eye/gold coin. Ten bright eyes, six thousand dollars/scepters, equaled one ingot bar.

Thus, my currency system was created: 30, 20, 10, and 1.

Have you created a system for your world? What does it look like? Is it easy or complicated? The beauty about creating my world is I now have a foundation, and any other monetary system I create can piggyback off the first. Less work in the end, and I'm all for saving time.

So, in short, streamline where you can, and spend the time where you can't. No matter how much or little you world build, whether before or during the manuscript process, always take notes. Save them somewhere that you can find in a hurry for quick reference instead of buried within your text. Copy the essential lines out of your story, and paste them elsewhere. Okay, let's move on to another method.

The World of Three Whys

The three whys is something I've heard about several times, but I can't tell you where. The concept is pretty simple and runs along the same lines of my thought process. Too much depth into something is time wasted, and the reader won't care.

The three whys stem from the question: why? You get to ask why at the end of each explanation before you stop. Any further is considered unnecessary. Here's an example:

My main character's name is Lana.

Why?

She was named after her grandmother.

Why?

Her grandmother was a famous healer during the goblin wars.

Why?

Instead of staying home as a young wife, she followed her husband to the front and treated many soldiers. She saved many lives and was hailed a hero.

And now you stop. Any more digging won't be beneficial, as the reader is following the story of the granddaughter Lana, not the grandmother. Unless young Lana molds all her life choices after her ancestor and is trying to follow in her footsteps, creating too much backstory won't help and is unnecessary.

This is one of the simplest and most straightforward methods for world-building. Have you ever tried this method?

Other Means of World Building

Do you possess a map of your world? One of the first things I did when I woke up from that fevered dream in my early twenties was to draw a map. Once I realized I was going to forget names and locations, my poor artistry skills were flexed. Many people doodle little sketches of their world as a means of fleshing out the places.

Another approach is to imagine your current society, take elements, and change aspects until it's unrecognizable. History is replete with bizarre events, and there's plenty to incorporate. Plus, drawing from history is a great way to outline where you want your story to go with minor course corrections based upon your changes. *Game of Thrones* is loosely based upon past events.

Also, in terms of bizarre, you can look up news articles, and I can almost guarantee that nothing you come up with will match the crazy within the paper. Do a quick search of Florida man and a date, and I'm sure you'll stumble across something.

You can pull inspiration from other novels and movies, just make sure you don't lift wholesale. It's impossible to be original nowadays, so instead, you should be shooting for unique. Brandon Sanderson's *Mistborn* trilogy stands out in its magic systems. Granted, I'm not a devourer of books, but I've never run across anything remotely close. Maybe I'm not as widely read as some, or perhaps it's relatively original?

You can also try mixing and matching genres, one example is the TV series *Firefly*. It's a sci-fi with a splash of the rugged, old western vibe thrown into the mix. The characters were all distinctive, and most were tethered together by a few causes.

Is magic in your story? How has this changed your society? In the *Dark Legacy* series, magic is prevalent, and technology has ground to a halt. There's no need when spellcraft can do almost everything. Yes, they charge, it is a commodity after all.

Want to visit family half a continent away? You can either do the old-fashioned horses and wagon, and it'll take you weeks or months to get there, or you can pay for a porting stone and arrive instantaneously. They don't need cars or airplanes. Want to talk to a relative? You can FaceTime them with a mirror and some conjury. Be sure when you incorporate something as life-changing as the mystics account for global impact.

Another way to set your world apart is the plant and animal life. Does your book deal with those elements? What about a culture within your realm? Do they clash with another society over plants and animals? Take another step further in sci-fi. What kind of aliens are out there? How are they different from *Star Trek* and *Star Wars*?

Languages are a part of our world, and they should be in yours. If you're not a linguist, I don't expect you to build your own language, but they can at least have a name. Further, if your MC is listening to people converse, describe the sounds.

Religion. Numerous books have beliefs within, some distinguished and others not so much. Do they play a significant part in your world? You can look at the tenents of our planet and try to construct distinct differences between them. It's a good starting point, but once you've outlined differences, deep dive and flesh them out. Does a character come from a culture where religion is a prominent staple in their life? How does living/traveling with the people of your story challenge them?

What kind of infrastructure supports your world? What kind of government and social classes make up your societies? Is the value or worth of someone passed upon the almighty coin, shard plate, or magical abilities? Or perhaps it's the farmers as they produce all the food. Without them, people die, and folks come to pay homage to those essential workers.

Again, I say craft with caution. If it never comes up in your story, why world-build? If you want notes for yourself so you understand your setting better, then do so. I encourage you to do this. I write many things that never make the final book, but I have it should I find the need or create future plots with the notes I've written. Many authors use this method when crafting characters, so why not steal for world-building purposes?

Your world's history is also important. Is the story of why we are following your character relevant to something in the past? If so, this *is* something your reader should know. You need to explain this in enough detail to show why it's important without getting bogged down. Is the setting a post-apocalyptic world? What caused the end of times? Imagine if the story of *Terminator* never delved into how or why Skynet became the killing machine mainframe. How odd would that be? Would the story even be close to the same without that element?

Some authors use soft writing in sci-fi. They don't explain the technology but focus on other elements of the story. The tech aids the narrative, but not as a prominent focal point. Have you thought about incorporating this approach?

Here's something to keep in mind: if you are writing a series or a trilogy, you don't have to relay *everything* upfront. You've got time to peel back in layers. Make your mark in the first book, and expand in subsequent stories. It's okay for readers to be left with questions left unanswered at the end. That'll make them want to continue reading in the next. With all the answers, they can guess the ending. Why continue reading?

What makes your world/story exemplary? Once you have the answer, build off that single notion. Flesh it out, give it a life of its own. Know it, breathe it, live it. Immerse uniqueness into the culture, and create strange or alien societal norms. You've got to make your mark in your world, so what is it, and how can the reader become lost?

Chapter 5: Creating Flawed, Memorable Characters

Emphasis on Character

This segment will be quite robust. I believe characters make or break a story. Ever watch a so-so movie, but the cast was fantastic? The emotional punch of the film comes from the reactions and stresses centered around a character? Did you tear up watching Christopher Nolan's *Interstellar* when the father, Cooper, drove away from his daughter? And then, she came running out after him? The scene hits me every time, and while a plot element, if you had no connection to the individual, I dare say you wouldn't have had such an emotional reaction.

Nolan is a master of character, no matter what the movie is about. The *Batman* trilogy, *Prestige, Inception, Interstellar, Memento, Insomnia*—all are phenomenal in establishing characters. And this, above all, I hope you take from this book.

Character over plot wins every time.

You can have a masterful storyline and terrible characters, and you'll fall flat. Readers are ruthless when it comes to dissecting your work, so let's not give them a reason to hunt for more flaws, unless, of course, they are diving deep into why your flawed cast was so meaningful to them, and how relatable they are.

And that is the key: relatable. Keep this in mind as we go through the next sessions.

Iconic Roles

A story needs a setting and a plot. I think of setting as the vehicle. It can be slick, beautifully-crafted, and gleam in the sunlight, but that's all it is, a frame. The plot is the fuel, the element which gets everything started and keeps it going. And while all this is a start, there's no interior to the vehicle, no engine, no place to sit.

In my head, this is your character. A shiny exterior will do nothing. Yes, it might get looks, but when a buyer comes closer to inspect and sees nothing within, they'll walk away. How do you keep your buyers—readers —from walking away? Great characters.

Generally speaking, your audience will forgive you for having a mediocre story as long as your characters deliver. Think back to the movies you've watched. Which one(s) made the story? Quite a few come to mind. You can name them, and their images pop out at you long after you've last seen the film.

The Joker: *The Dark Knight*
Darth Vader: *Original Star Wars* Trilogy
Sarah Connor: *Terminator 1 & 2*
Samwise Gamgee: *LOTR* trilogy
Hannibal Lecter: *The Silence of the Lambs*
The Man with No Name: *The Good, the Bad, and the Ugly*
Ellen Ripley: *Alien*
Thanos: *Infinity War*
Indiana Jones

If you've never watched the movies listed above, you've at least heard of them. More to the point, I bet you know their appearance by sight. They're iconic. Whether they've shown up as memes or the most quoted lines ever, that's the power of their performance, the potential of character. This translates to your story.

You may not be able to build a world like Pandora in *Avatar* or have the vision of George Lucas to create the next *Star Wars*, but you can craft the next Ellen Ripley or Samwise Gamgee. Why did I pick these two out of all the others listed above? Because these are the most relatable, and they resonate with the audience.

Everyone wants a friend like Sam, to help you up the steps of Mount Doom, and remain loyal to the end. Everyone wishes they were brave like Ripley, to face down something from nightmares and have the courage to save a little girl from the clutches of death. If only we could be so selfless.

We don't relate to them by the traits they exhibit, but that we wish we had that in ourselves and in others. But what of those other iconic portrayals mentioned above.

There's something quite disturbing when we first meet Hannibal Lecter. Clarice walks down the hall, seeing all the other insane inmates, and we prepare for the worst—only to find Hannibal standing in the center of his cell.

What's more, there are long takes where he doesn't blink, which adds to the eerie effect. He's charming, well-mannered, educated in the fact that he was a psychiatrist. What snapped in him to make him murder and eat his victims? There's something tantalizing in the questions he raises—and in the desire to understand his psyche. Further, he's not the villain of the story; he's an antagonist.

Darth Vader, the most iconic persona for generations, was set up in his first entrance aboard Princess Leia's ship. His towering frame, black clothing, mechanical breathing, and deep rumbling voice added to his presence. All are iconic in their own way. Through Obi-Wan, Luke learns that his father, Anakin, was a Jedi and a friend, but murdered by a pupil of Kenobi's.

In *Empire Strikes Back (ESB)*, Luke faces the man who slew his father, only to learn his father is the infamous villain. But Vader isn't relatable. It isn't until *Return of the Jedi* (ROTJ) that we can empathize with him. More than that, we empathize with him through Luke, his son. And when he makes his critical choice to turn away from the dark side and save his son, we finally see the good in him.

What about the Joker? We don't relate to him at all, but we understand him, at least, we think we do. As an agent of chaos, we get the gist of his overall goal, but not the motivation. At Harvey Dent's bedside in the hospital, he tells us, "Do I really look like a guy with a plan?" He's a fractured but compelling character, and his performance is chilling.

What better antagonist than the unpredictable one? As Alfred aptly put it, "Because some men aren't looking for anything logical, like money. They can't be bought, bullied, reasoned, or negotiated with. Some men just want to watch the world burn."

How would all these movies turn out if those characters hadn't been well written and compelling? Whether a villain or hero, characters make or break a story. In this section, we'll deep dive into one of the most essential segments in presenting a story.

Archetypes

There are many places to start on a character. In the following sections, we'll cover archetypes, Myers-Briggs, and enneagrams.

Archetypes are found in almost every story. Even if the author didn't intentionally write the characters as such, they do tend to slip into roles. There are many versions of the archetypes and some mix and match as needed. Depending on who you ask, there can be a few to several. Some split up the hero into another segment called the leader. I can see the logic, but I'm not one for overcomplicated things. So, let's stick with the basics.

Archetypes embody elements of mankind and our struggle with life and set characters on a path of behaviors. They can also represent the good and evil in others who've at one point or another, crossed our path, and the reactions to the environment reinforce the archetype.

The Hero. Each story typically starts out with them in their routine life before heeding the call of adventure, and proving to themselves and others their worth. Typically, the audience sees through this character's eyes as the journey unfolds. Luke Skywalker, Harry Potter, and Alita follow this archetype.

The Mentor. Each hero needs a mentor, someone to push them on their way, give them a fighting chance, and then typically disappears. Gandalf, Dumbledore, and Obi-Wan Kenobi fill this part.

The Guardian, also known as Threshold Guardian, shows up to test the hero in some way, often blocking the protagonist's path. They can appear at any part of the story, and there can be more than one.

Heralds. Those filling this role show up at the beginning and urge change in some shape or manner. More often than not, they don't have a presence other than this and often fade into the background, but not always. Objects can also be heralds. R2-D2 and Harry's Hogwarts letter are heralds.

Shapeshifters often blur the line between friend and foe. They can go as far as to betray the hero or the group to achieve something they want. Even if they don't, tension can arise among the group's interpersonal relationships and be tested in many ways. Captain Jack Sparrow and Severus Snape, both whom play their role differently, are iconic.

Shadows are the villains of the story—whether the main antagonist or not—and challenge the hero and give them purpose. Like a herald, they can be embodied by a character or something intangible or supernatural. Darth Vader, Terminator, and Thanos are shadows, and they cast long ones at that.

The Trickster can often be seen as comic relief, but more than that, they upset the status quo and offer an outsider's perspective to the happenings of the story. Deadpool, Loki, and Bugs Bunny, are tricksters.

An important note: your characters can shift from one personification to another as needed, and you can present more than one per story. Yoda and Kenobi are both mentors to Luke. There are more archetypes, but these are the primary ones. You can go more in-depth, but too far, and you're splitting hairs. In my book, *The Bearer of Secrets*, Judas fulfills the role of mentor, but I didn't set out to write him as such; he just slipped into it. Characters can be crafted in many different ways, and this is but one. Let's move on to another.

Myers-Briggs

The Myers-Briggs is another method for creating characters, specifically when looking at their sixteen personality types. It must be noted that the intent is not to determine which is better, but more to quantify a person and help them understand themselves. We can, and many have used this as a basis to create deeper characters than those based upon a role.

The sixteen personality types are broken down by assessments of strengths, weaknesses, likes, and dislikes through the quiz. There are eight total traits.

The first two form a dichotomy that covers how people interact with the world around them.

1: Extraversion—E—the more outgoing type, enjoys socializing.

2: Introversion—I—prefers time alone and enjoys deep, meaningful interactions.

The second group covers how people collect information about the world around them.

3: Sensing—S—pays more attention to reality and focuses on facts and details.

4: Intuition—N—pays more attention to patterns and impressions, thinks about abstract theories and imagines the future.

The third group informs how people come about making a decision.

5: Thinking—T—A significant focus is placed upon objective data and facts, often resulting in a logical decision.

6: Feeling—F—Those who fall under the feeling trait consider other people and their emotions before reaching a decision.

The last two deal more with how people handle the outside world.

7: Judging—J—if decisive conclusions and structure sound more like you, then this trait is yours.

8: Perceiving—P—If you ever met someone who is adaptable and capable of change, they may fall under this category.

From these eight traits, we arrive at sixteen personalities. There are numerous websites that go in-depth on what each personality type means. For a bit of fun, if you haven't already, take their quiz.

Remember: there's no right or wrong answer, just answer with the truth, and you'll have your personality type at the end.

I've taken the test, and my personality type is INTJ, and this one is referred to as the architect or strategist. One interesting fact I found is that roughly 1-4% of the population is INTJ. Let's break down the personality type and see what we come up with.

Without a doubt, I'm an introvert, and I'd rather be by myself than out socializing. The best way for me to recharge is to go home and relax. I do tend to focus on the abstract, big picture, but put emphasis on logic and objective information. And to make sure I'm orderly, I do plan out things well in advance, especially time off or vacations.

But a personality isn't anything without strengths and weaknesses. According to the results, my strengths are: theoretical concepts, high expectations, good listener, takes criticism well—I'll be honest, depends on the circumstance—hardworking, and confident.

Now for the juicy weaknesses: overly analytical, judgmental, perfectionist—this is true without a doubt!—talking about emotions makes me uncomfortable, and I often come across as insensitive and callous; this last part is also definitely true!

What I find interesting about this personality type, according to the results, is that I don't care about what people think, but I care about their emotions. Also, according to the results, I fit with other real and fictitious people: Thomas Jefferson, Arnold Schwarzenegger, C. S. Lewis, and Gandalf.

So, are you going to take the quiz? What do you think your results will be? Does this sound like an interesting avenue to pursue making characters? On to the next way to build characters.

Enneagrams

Here is another exciting way to create characters. There are nine enneagrams, all arranged in a circle and crisscrossed with other personality types.

1: The Perfectionist: they go about correcting wrongs with honesty, dependability, and common sense. With high standards to be taken seriously, they leave no room for someone else's point of view (POV).

2: The Helper: a feeling-based individual who empathizes, supports, and brings out the best in everyone. They have a problem setting personal boundaries and are often overrun by emotional pressure and seek acceptance.

3: The Performer: another feeling-based type, taps into this strength to get things done with initiative and adaptability. With no time to slow down and an image to maintain, they've got to figure out what's vital for them.

4: The Romantic: another feeler prone to melancholy, so they may seek a quest to find their missing link. Meaningful relationships are their cornerstone, but they need time alone. Finding a balance between happiness and sadness is a must to thrive.

5: The Observer: an intellectual of analytical perception with a penchant for autonomy. Though brilliant of mind, relationships befuddle these folks.

6: Loyal Skeptic: an intellect who focuses on guarding the safety of those around them. Though ready with a solution to never-ending problems, they doubt themselves and hate procrastination.

7: The Epicure: an optimist who prefers unlimited possibilities and the option for fun while moving forward. Communication is never an issue with these intellectuals, but their attention wanes quickly, and the moment at hand is lost on them.

8: The Protector: a body-based type who seems born to be the leader and seeks out justice and fairness. Despite this, there's little patience for rules, and they'll often do things their own way with energy and an intimidating intensity.

9: The Mediator: the ninth persona located at the top of the circles, these types are seen as balanced, as are their views. If the others are body parts, nine is the blood flowing through it. With attention shifts and failure to stick with priorities, they sometimes come across as out of touch.

I've never personally created MCs from enneagrams, but I have made minor or smaller, recurring characters from them. The beauty of this method is their personalities give you a lot to draw from with relative ease and without deep diving. However, like the archetypes, making a character based upon a role can have limitations, so when it comes to MCs, I tend to stick with my own method, which we'll start discussing next.

How I Build Characters

When building a house, you make plans, pour the slab, add the frame and roof, and do the interior. In essence, you build from the ground up and outside in. Many people take this approach to creating characters, or at the very least, use a template that acts as a frame. I don't. Since this is a fictional character, I can craft them however I want and in whatever order I choose. So, I work from the inside out.

But why, you might ask. Simple. Characters are more than their looks, they are more than a role they fill in a story. They aren't defined by a singular trait such as appearance, what group they identify with, where they were born, religion, or sexuality. They're people, and we've got to view them as such. Think of your story as history that's already happened, and you're getting to reveal it to the world. These people have lived, breathed, and died, and we get to show them but a sliver of who they were.

Thinking back on people who made their mark in history—they were greater than the average person, and so must our characters be.

Hopefully, by the time these next few segments are concluded, you'll appreciate this method.

Part 1—The Foundation

I've heard a lot of people talk about how they interview their characters. My first question is, how? My second question would be why. Judging by everything you've read so far in this book, do you need to know your character's favorite color? It depends on whether it comes up or not in the book. If it doesn't, then the answer is no.

As for the *how* in the pre-building stage, I don't even know my character well enough to flesh out who they are or what they look like, so how can I ask them, "Hey, bro, what's your favorite pizza?" First off, there isn't pizza in my world, so it's an irrelevant question. Most of those questionnaires online don't develop the character's depth wholesale; ergo, a waste of time.

Other times, folks will build their characters based upon one specific trait. While this can be good if you want to set them in a place of an unfamiliar setting, like a centaur among the goblin masses, their depth tends to be rather shallow, lacking in the elements that make a remarkable person.

There's more to people than appearance, ideological beliefs, religion, ethnicity, or upbringing. To define a person, let alone a fictional person you're building, based on one of these traits, sells the character, reader, and person short of the justice they deserve.

I once sent a cousin an early draft of my first novel. He dutifully read it and handed it back with notes. The most significant criticism he had was that my characters were flat. This had been a first, but I vowed for it to be the last. I did a deep dive into characters in general and found a fundamental flaw in all of them. There wasn't a template from which to build anyone.

Granted, I later found Myers-Briggs and enneagrams, to which I've amended my ways, but when you look at the hero archetype, there really isn't any substance to their core. The template says to be a hero, they need these traits. And that didn't sit well with me.

So, I started thinking, what's something everyone has in common, no matter what ethnicity, upbringing, financial background, country origin, or time period? And when the answer came, I laughed. You'll laugh, too, roll your eyes, and think I'm absurd, but hear me out. The commonality is zodiacs.

This isn't a call for believing fortune tellings or horoscopes. I couldn't tell you what the planets mean with this one is rising, and this one is … free-falling? I don't know any of that, but zodiacs give you five to eight positive and negative traits to each sign. Let's hit the pause button real quick.

Storytime: In college, I did a paper on zodiacs. This was during the years I discovered this as an excellent means for making characters. I did a survey with the class, some of whom were honest and others not so much. Here's what I found.

Generally speaking, about 70% of the zodiac is accurate for all people. This is a large margin of error, but what they don't account for is life events, personal choices, free will, financial freedom, upbringing, societal mores, and religion.

But to write this persuasive paper, I had to do research. Here's what I found: ancient Babylonians, Sumerians, Hindu, Chinese, Greeks, Romans, Mayans, Egyptians, and numerous other countries had them from their earliest inceptions as nations. For thousands of years, people have been looking at the stars, plotting their course, charting how seasons and months affect us. When I sit and think of it in that manner, I find it fascinating and mind-boggling.

Aristotle studied astronomy, anatomy, zoology, physics, and metaphysics. He also had a robust understanding of theology, psychology, and geology, to name a few. Plato, one of the world's best-known philosophers, was Socrates's student and the teacher of Aristotle. He wrote in the middle of the fourth century B.C. and also studied astronomy. And Socrates? You remember him, right? He was a great Greek philosopher who created Socratic irony and the Socratic method.

What do Plato, Socrates, and Aristotle have in common?

They believed in the Circle of Animals. Astronomy and Astrology were of the same science in ancient times. Astrology seeks the meaning and application of the influences of the planets, stars, and other celestial phenomena. Astronomy is the science of mapping the positions and movements of heavenly bodies and other elements beyond the Earth's atmosphere.

So, with the little history lesson over, let's continue.
Zodiacs.
With the knowledge I imparted about why I believe in a 30% margin of error, what do you think? Is it plausible? What's your zodiac? In the last chapter of the book, I'll be listing the zodiacs, and I want you to be honest with yourself when you read it. Is it you? Are small portions missing? Do some seem partially correct?

We don't have to worry about 100% accuracy with zodiacs and fictitious people; we just need a foundation to pull from. This is where we employ your artistic license. We've got to make a base our readers can relate to, but picking a zodiac won't make them rounded. They're layered, complex people like everyone else.

Since I'm an Aries, I'm going to pick the Aries zodiac to start building. For this, I want to use a little bit of imagination to go along with this example. Think of this character we are developing as a blank template, a mannequin, a faceless individual with unspecified sex.

Note: if you're writing a story about a single woman in a setting of only men, or a human (specific race) living in a civilization with only goblins, it's okay to go ahead and select your sex and race. However, if you're not doing something so specific, leave them a blank canvas. After we've built this template, I want to show you how awesome your character can be regardless of race, ethnicity, or sex.

The Aries zodiac:

Positive: Adventurous and energetic; pioneering and courageous; enthusiastic and confident; dynamic and quick-witted.

Negative: Selfish; quick-tempered; impulsive; impatient; foolhardy; and daredevil.

For the most part, I'd say this almost defines me to a T. I'm not so much a daredevil to put myself in harm's way. I don't go bungee jumping, but I will be daring if what I say will upset someone. I don't mind ruffling feathers. I'll probably go ahead and say it before thinking. This is the quick wit and impulsiveness playing their parts.

I digress.

Now, let's build for a trilogy set in ancient times, and you want one character to be a soldier in the army. This is your first book, so we don't want to be too detailed. Right now, let's pick two positive and two negative traits. In a sequel, you can add a third to explore more in-depth. Knowing this, you can even foreshadow those elements of their foundation. However, let's not get distracted.

Judging from the lists above, does anything call to you? What combination would make a conflicted person? For the positive, let's go with confidence and quick-witted, and for the negative, let's pull quick-tempered and impulsive. Can you see an internal conflict arising from my choices? If yes, you are on the right track.

So, we've got a character in the army, a sword-wielding soldier, who's not in charge, but a position or two away from the top rank of their squad. Can any conflicts arise from this circumstance? How would this play against the power position in their team?

Do you remember when I talked about foreshadowing other things about them? Let's foreshadow courageous, too. Do you think this MC we are creating is going to be content with staying in the number three spot? Or will they want to rise above? How will your MC react to taking orders, especially ones they see as wrong? Will they obey, or will they break rank and try to outshine them all?

Let's move on to the next part of building characters.

Part 2—Motivation Based on Real Aspects

This next aspect will most likely polarize readers. Everyone—well, almost everyone—wants their hero or villain to be memorable in some form or another, and most mistake "unforgettable" for the nobility of cause or a menacing aura. We'll break this down, but for now, let's explore some unique characters.

Remember: this is my interpretation of the characters we're talking about. You may see something different. That's what makes people, characters, and art unique, the different opinions and views based upon a subjective inspection.

The first book character that comes to mind is Harry Potter. What's remarkable about him, besides he's the chosen one marked by Voldemort? He possesses no extraordinary powers of the magical kind. He's not Dumbledore. So, what's special about him?

In my mind, specifically in the last few chapters of *Harry Potter and the Goblet of Fire* as Voldemort returned (when the book came out way back then), and in *Harry Potter and the Deathly Hallows*, Harry seemed to be at his weakest or at least, vulnerable. I thought Harry's going to die, despite the series being named after him, which implies survival. To be fair, when I read *Goblet*, I didn't realize it was supposed to be a longer series. I was just reading it on a challenge from a ten-year-old.

Moving to the silver screen, the first is a villain, Darth Vader. This figure is dressed in black with a long flowing cape, kills subordinates for failure, chops off his son's hand, and tries to recruit him to the dark side. Despite not winning Employee of the Year or expecting anything for Father's Day, he's quite significant with his rhythmic breathing, deep, resonant voice, and towering frame. And that's not mentioning his artifact, the thrum of his red lightsaber.

For a TV show, two characters are Daenerys Targaryen and Arya Stark. One is remembered for her long, platinum blonde hair and the mother of dragons; the other for her journey from a daughter of House Stark to one of the Faceless Men. There is a plethora of reasons why each is infamous, be it quirky lines, tongue in cheek humor, internal conflicts, or decisions that make us cringe.

So, what is our MC's focus? In books or movies, I've always responded more to a focal point grounded in reality. *The Dark Knight* trilogy is an excellent example of grounding into reality. It's *Batman*, a comic book incarnation, a human with superb intellect and physical conditioning, but human nonetheless. In this incarnation, he relied on gadgets and technology, something a real Batman would need. Although some might still be unachievable, his technology is grounded in rules we understand. In a sense, the trilogy gave us a 'real' example of Batman.

So, how does this apply to our character's focus and story? Here is the polarizing effect: I argue our lead and/or supporting cast will be more memorable if your reader can relate to something visceral and familiar. To me, there are a handful of main categories, though there are more: money, power, sex, family, religion, adventure/freedom, and survival.

In the simplest of forms, these factors drive the world today. Not everyone will be motivated by the above, but you can find their focus in other things. Let's do a breakdown here.

Almost everyone is influenced, in one way or the other, by the sway of the dollar. We need money to pay for essentials and other items falling under the 'wants' category. We want a nice retirement, a roomy house, a newer car to provide for our family. Is this what's driving our MC— material wealth? Han Solo exemplifies this in *SW: A New Hope*, where he takes on desperate passengers Obi-Wan Kenobi and Luke Skywalker. He's looking for a payout to get out from under Jabba's thumb. If our MC is swimming in money like Bruce Wayne, then it's not a motivating factor.

Power is the next application. Almost every story is this in some form, manipulation, means, magical, mythical, or majestic. You rarely find heroes drawn to it, but they do exist. Darth Vader is a prime example of a power-driven individual. He's second in the Empire but has aspirations of overthrowing the emperor. He went as far as to recruit his son to help him.

The Mother of Dragons in *Game of Thrones* is another prime example of a power-driven role, which doesn't make her bad. She wants her ancestral throne in the seven kingdoms and freedom for all slaves and the suppressed. She has an army, ships, dragons, and intent, but will she capitalize on it?

Remember: there are many types of power: superpowers, tyrannical, political, corporate, financial, domineering... the list is almost endless. I'm leaving this unanswered, as season eight turned out to be a dud, and Martin has yet to write the ending.

Sex. The taboo subject for most Americans. It's expected, as the American culture was built on puritan views centuries ago. Those who are not driven by the first two we discussed often find themselves in this arena. For those having reached the pinnacles of authority and money with little else to achieve may crave a new type of prestige. A business tycoon purchasing another company is a way of expanding their base, or a governor running for president. I'm sure you've heard the tales about CEOs who seek the company of a dominatrix.

In the real world, CEOs hold all the power, but they give up their claim in a dominatrix's presence. I've heard it's a way to relieve stress, but I wouldn't know, as I have neither that much wealth nor the accompanying clout. You could use this as a time to do some hands-on character research if you wanted. All jokes aside, sex may not be involved in the dominatrix's thrall, but they may be entering a realm where the lines become blurred.

Maybe our MC is dying for affection and was often the object of ridicule while growing up. No woman would *ever* love him, so he must pay for affection. You also have the men and women who are players of the field, and they find gratification in picking up an unsuspecting mark at a bar, club, etc. Is our MC driven by this? It's okay if they are. If anything, it makes them far more interesting because the first two choices are the most typical.

The focal point of a family can be extended to close friends. If you have no family, your best friends fill this gap. Harry Potter and Arya Stark fall into this category in one aspect or another. And yes, they can have more than one. Harry has lost his mom and dad and never knew them. Ron and Hermione make up his new family. Arya Stark is driven by the loss of her father and revenge. Family compels both of them, but though they share a commonality, how far do they diverge from one another? Who says family can't be an attractive choice?

Religion and other focuses. If our MC is a warrior and religious, obviously, this might be the logical choice, but you may want to shift attention from piety to wrestle with codes against sex, violence, and material wealth.

Remember: your audience can relate to each of these in one form or another, but they may not to his prayers for strength. Does our MC keep to the path, or does the Jezebel in the next town over make them falter? As stated before, you can have others, but the further you move from the core, the more obscured it becomes to your reader.

So, what classification does our MC fall into? Their category can be the antithesis of what you just read. Perhaps they could be a tyrant or a benevolent emperor, and the struggle is to fight the impulse to rule because people who should be free?

All our characters in a book can have the motivation for power but in different types. A lot of these go hand in hand, so don't discard one because you don't like it. Push yourself out of the comfort zone and write something masterful.

For this section and our MC, we'll go with power/authority. Let's move on to the next part.

Part 3—Internal Desires, Personality, & Moral Code

Internal desires are a stark contrast to their foundational traits and motivation. The zodiac we selected is meant to show how they will act/react to the world around them. The motivation is their end goal. Now, let's throw all of that out of whack by giving two internal desires. Again, you can have more, but remember, this is the first book.

Ideally, you want these to conflict in a significant way, pulling them apart to two drastic ends. You can pick two that are closer together at first glance, but there must be a distinction, a breaking point.

> **Storytime**: In my first book, *The Bearer of Secrets*, one of the main protagonists, the exiled warlock, Judas Lakayre, has two desires: to be lawfully obedient and to be morally right. At first glance, these seem to be the same, but they're not. In the story, he obeys the law even though he's an exile. This is a moral decision that backs up the first. However, when the same government gives him an immoral order, expecting him to obey, he rebels. What was the order? To return a girl back to her world, which would end up killing her. Now, he is morally right, preserving her life, but unlawful in his disobedience—those two dynamics wreak havoc on him throughout the story.

So, what two desires will we give our MC? Perhaps they want to be religious and follow the covenants of their deity, which forbids killing, but the MC also strives to be the best soldier. Maybe they seek to leave the service but are confident that if they do, the MC's fellow soldiers will die.

Or it can be something both simple and robust—to be the best soldier and to want a family, but living a soldier's life isn't ideal for children or a relationship in ancient times. Will the internal war reach a precipice? These passions must reach a culmination in which a choice is made one way or another, unless, of course, the decision is taken from them.

Let's assume because they've chosen to be a soldier, they want to be the best. And, let's give them the desire for a family or a meaningful connection. Now, let's recap: confident and quick-witted, impulsive and quick-tempered, driven by power, seeking to be the best soldier and to have a meaningful relationship.

That's a lot in one package. You can go so many ways with this character already, and you haven't gotten to the plot. Or perhaps there's a premise already and you're building characters to match your story. Either way, the plethora of options available is astounding.

Now, let's give our mannequin a personality!

Is our MC snarky and sarcastic, genuine and pleasant, talks in a soft voice or strident tones? Introverted or extroverted? Mayhaps a combination of both? What about a romantic interest? Is it budding or withering? Are they happy or disgruntled, both professionally and personally? If you don't know what kind of personality to give them or don't want to take the time, you can find one in the Myers-Briggs foundation.

Remember: these are your characters, and you can pull from any template to get the desired effect.

Our MC is quick-witted, so let's make them snarky and sarcastic. Since they're motivated by power, let's throw a twist in it and make them an introvert. How does that dynamic play out down the road? Disgruntled by their position and always feeling the urge to take charge—to outshine everyone—will they leave the comforting bubble of their introverted shell?

Since they desire a meaningful relationship, they're still single. Again, introverted nature plays against them. Furthermore, since they are quick-tempered, everyone is cautious about approaching the MC for a relationship.

Let's move to the next part: moral code and beliefs. These I use interchangeably. You can build another layer of complexity to your character or keep it simple. By now, we've added a great deal of depth to our mannequin.

Can someone be religious, quick-tempered, and also an adventurous extrovert? What about confident, agnostic, and an impulsive introvert? Any combination is possible. Do they think killing is okay during wartime, but cold-blooded murder isn't? What internal or external guidance directs our character's actions on a moral, religious, or creed basis? These are questions you should ponder. If you don't know, that's fine.

Remember: this is the first book, and like world-building, you don't need all the answers. Maybe over the course of writing, this will be revealed to you.

One last bit to make your characters more compelling or dynamic is love languages and how they use them. How do they interact? For me, I need to receive words of affirmation, but I give or send love through quality time spent with the significant other and gifts. How will this play out among your cast? How can this dynamic add extra twists?

Let's move on to the last section of how I create characters.

Part 4—Features

Features are the last on my list. Why? Because I build from the inside out. We're sitting on a complex, flawed person with unlimited potential. For features, I'm not referring to eye color, hair color, or ethnicity. I'm talking about scars, tattoos, and deformities. Does our MC have a tattoo? If so, what does it look like, and what's the story behind it?

In the planning stages, you don't need all the answers. Sometimes writing a few chapters will bring a character to life for you. Another factor to keep in mind is not to reveal everything on the first go-around. No info dumps. Maybe our mannequin has a tattoo of a dragon on the right shoulder, but the story isn't revealed until the second novel.

Foster intrigue with our MC. What does the dragon tattoo look like? A green dragon head wreathed in flame. That short description is enough for someone to create a mental picture. You don't need to be detailed with what kind of needles, how intricate the craftsmanship was, or how long it took.

Or, imagine a segment of the MC's ear is missing from a knife fight. Does the right eye sit a little lower than the left? Though the initial impulse is to make our characters beautiful, not everyone in your novel can be a model. It's okay to have a good-looking man or woman, even a couple of them. Are they around for our MC to become envious or covetous? Always give them a flaw, even the beautiful, perfect ones.

Storytime: In a sequel to my main series, I created a prostitute named Joy. She's the epitome of beauty in every manner, as I intended her to be, except one. Her nose is bulbous with a horrendous, bent shape to it, and she often thinks of it as a vulture's beak. Those words alone invoke such a sharp mental picture. And despite the nose, she's sought after by numerous customers, but there's another flaw. People call her Joy because she's never happy. In fact, she often cries, which ruins the mood for her customers. The emotions are powerful and amplified by magic she didn't know she had.

What am I saying? Even the most beautiful people are flawed, especially if unseen. A man or woman who is a perfect ten can be the biggest monster in the privacy of their home. Show this. Make your characters flawed. Flaws are real, and your characters should possess them, too.

With a solid idea about our MC's core, and the beginning stages of what their exterior is like, we start to get a picture.

Recap: confident and quick-witted, impulsive and quick-tempered, driven by power, seeking to be the best soldier with a meaningful relationship. This snarky and sarcastic introvert has a tattoo of a green dragon on the left shoulder and is missing a chunk at the top of the right ear. This is an engaging, complex, layered, flawed individual, and all without ever determining the ethnicity, sex, or, in the case of a fantasy genre, race (goblin, dwarf, elf).

It's time to choose the sex.

Let's make our MC female and a goblin. That's pretty sweet, especially if this person is in a setting where there are only humans around her. Better yet, we can read about this fantastic character from the point of view (POV) of an enemy combatant. She's on the bad guy's side. That's a punch to the gut.

We've laid out so many ways this individual is relatable, and it doesn't matter her outward appearance or that she's the enemy. A well-written character is relatable, and I bet by the end of the book, you can make your reader cheer for her, too.

How does our female goblin warrior appear? Is she tall, short, voluptuous, curvy, skinny, fat, or athletic? Long legs with a short torso or just the opposite? What kind of lips? Full, downward turned, heart-shaped, thin lips, or uneven? What about her nose? Is it snubbed, bulbous, celestial, aquiline, or broken? Perhaps the ridge of the nose is tall and makes her eyes appear deeper than what they are. Her eyebrows? Eye shape and color? Hair color and length. Is it wavy, curly, straight, fine, thick?

Now, imagine you were trying to do that to a human female. All the questions should be the same when determining appearance. Guys, too. You may think this is too detailed, but it's not. You can add these little snippets throughout a few pages to paint a mural of their appearance and how they are. There are still elements to discuss, like body shape.

Is she tall, short, average height? What's her best physical feature? What aspects of her physicality, mentality, emotionality, and personality draw others? What part of her does she hate? What is a turn-off for others? There's an endless well to choose from.

To me, the hair, eye color, and ethnicity are trivial matters in the grand scheme—if you were making a human. These aspects I decide almost last unless I'm building a particular being or race from a segment of my world. That's the exterior packaging, which is minimal compared to the depth of the identity.

Our little goblin won't define herself based on the length of her legs or if she had frizzy hair. No, she's going to base herself on her beliefs, moral code, motivation, internal desires, and the traits/role she embodies. She's going to judge her caliber as a soldier by the incompetentce of the people around her.

So, what do you think? Is this a layered and interesting person? Regardless of race, sex, or ethnicity, let your character speak to you. There are a thousand ways to build, and this is but one. Take out what works for you and file away the portions that don't, but don't discard them. You never know when your next protagonist will come knocking.

My Character-Building Template

Below is a bare-bones character template to help you build memorable, flawed characters. Steal it. Use it. It's here for you to use.

Character Building Template

Focus Traits: Start with zodiac—choose one. Select two positive and negative traits.

Motivation: Focus on real aspects: money, sex, power, religion, family —notoriety, fame, infamy, survival, etc.

Desires: Try to pick them in opposite directions. This is the internal conflict.

Personality: Snarky, dry, dark, sarcastic? Pick 2–5 ways you can sprinkle this in your writing with action, dialogue, internal thought, clothing choice, religion, jewelry, etc.

From here, everything is secondary in my opinion (unless specifically building a character from a particular social standing, race or ethnicity, or locale).

Features: Height, weight, hair color, eye color, eyebrows, nose, lips, chin, face shape. What is his/her best physical feature? What aspects of his/her physicality, mentality, emotional availability, or personality draw others? What part of him/her does he/she hate? What is a turn-off for others?

Body Shape: Athletic, skinny, fat, voluptuous? Long Legs & short torso? Short legs & Long torso? Lanky arms? Long feet, wide feet? Bony hands? Fat fingers? Narrow hands, wide shoulders...

Secondary Features: Scars, tattoos, sound of their voice (how they talk/sound), mannerisms—tics (I usually do 2–5, depending on cast size.)

Ethnicity: What setting is your world? Earth? A fictitious world? Does this matter if you have chosen a goblin or an elf? How do the humans perceive the other races?

The All-Powerful MC

This should come as no surprise, but a main character who can do everything is boring. If your MC can achieve every part all on their own, why have side characters? As covered in this chapter, your MC should have flaws, and a part of that is their inability to accomplish everything without support. They need their companions to help them on their journey.

> **Storytime**: In the reviews to my first book, *The Bearer of Secrets*, I see one criticism more than any other, and that has to do with my MC, Julie. Most say she's unlikeable, or that she failed to deliver on the premise of being "all-powerful." Though this can be taken as a negative, I don't. Why? Because if she was all-powerful, she'd be boring to read.
>
> Instead, I wrote her on a reverse hero's journey, a subversion that everyone knows. Yes, she makes progress, becomes powerful, but at the end of the novel, she fails. In many ways, her story mirrors Luke Skywalker's in *ESB*, as he loses to Darth Vader. Taking a character in one book from knowing nothing of magic to defeating the bad guy is unrealistic. What if Luke overthrew the Empire in *SW: ANH*? Or what if Frodo destroyed the ring in his first movie? Would either of these make logical sense? I'd argue no.

Let's take a moment to talk about characters who need help in their goals and those who don't, and why I find them relatable or not.

The first one that comes to mind is Batman. Let's take *The Dark Knight* trilogy for the first example. Yes, Bruce Wayne is Batman, but what is Batman without his gadgets? In this incarnation, Bruce isn't the genius the comics portray. Moreover, he needs Lucius Fox to equip him with technology, both on the ground and above. Without Fox, Batman cannot be fully realized. Another point to bring up is the moral center the elder brings to the youthful vigilante.

Sticking with DC, let's look at the inverse: Superman. I know he's a fan favorite, the boy scout. He stands for truth, justice, and the American way. As a Kryptonian, he possesses numerous abilities thanks to our sun. With flight, superhuman speed and strength, X-ray vision, heat vision, super breath, and a plethora of others, one man can take on an entire legion of adversaries.

How can Superman ever be presented with a challenge? You've got to make even more powerful villains. The one crippling weakness is kryptonite, radioactive components from his home world. Without it, he's unstoppable, too powerful, and can easily—lacking a moral center—declare himself emperor of Earth.

Who are other too powerful characters? Do they have any weaknesses? Who can achieve their ends without the aid of companions? Are they a hero or a villain?

Thanos with the infinity gauntlet, Darkseid, Doomsday, Rey Palpatine, Optimus Prime, Neo, Wesley Crusher, Richard Rahl, Kaladin and Adolin, and Bella Swan.

So, what's the purpose of pointing out all these characters? Besides making them better with flaws, abilities that outstrip all those around them—whether physical, magical, or mental—can make your character boring. No one wants to read about a god who can do everything. And this is why I do not take the criticism of my MC too seriously. I didn't want her to be a god. She needs to build to that.

No one is so attractive that everyone they meet instantly falls in love with them. No one becomes best friends after one encounter. Superficial flaws aren't genuine, and they fall flat with your audience. Flaws should be drawbacks to your MC and hinder forward progression. One pep talk shouldn't have the power to erase something so ingrained. If any of these items make your checklist while crafting your character or story, revisions are needed.

Again, I pose the question: if your MC can do it all without the aid of a companion, why have side characters at all? Can your MC repair a ship they've never worked on, fly a ship, plot a course in space though they've never been there? What about speaking other languages? If your plot revolves around inserting a specific ability that only your hero can do and they've never attempted it before, it's time to go back to the drawing board. I'm looking at you Disney *Star Wars*.

Let's move on to Elements of Writing.

Chapter 6: Elements of Writing

My Rules on Writing

This next segment came about because I heard other published writers had rules they followed, not in the sense of the industry, but personal ones. And it got me thinking: what are my rules? What are lessons I learned along the way that shaped how I write now? So, I've come up with a few. We'll break them down after the list.

1: Set the tone, get to the point, and slow down—don't rush the small stuff.

2: Whittle, chisel, sculpt. Write it all, even stuff you won't need if it'll help you as an author, then butcher the hell out of it when editing.

3: Establish one of the following settings early in the story: physical, cultural, magical, spiritual, or morality (societal mores).

4: Ground your character in a relatable aspect: e.g., power, money, sex, religion, knowledge, family…

5: Don't control your characters or the story, let them go where they need.

6: When you're done writing, set it aside for a spell, and come back with fresh eyes.

1. *Set the tone, get to the point, and slow down*—Ambivalence isn't an enduring trait when setting up a story. Intrigue? Yes. Mystery? Absolutely. You want these elements, but not at the expense of toying with your reader.

Set the style with prose, character actions and reactions, dialogue, and setting. Setting plays a vital role. A story opening in a church gives a stark contrast to an opening in a brothel, a movie theater, or gladiatorial games. With tone, you are also indicating who your audience is meant to be. You don't want your adult novel falling into the hands of a young kid, who, not knowing, reads gore, violence, or sex-heavy scenes later. Hitting this from the start, your audience knows what they're in for and won't be surprised or turned off because you've warned them.

Prose can help nail this down. Later in this chapter, we'll talk about the first lines and the first chapter, but one example already establishes what kind of book it'll be. Gorgeously written, a touch artsy, but from the first sentence, there's a spirit embedded within.

Getting to the point is the inciting incident, the thing that kicks off the story. I try to put this as close to the front as possible. The longer the book, the more leeway you garner, but don't abuse your reader's goodwill. A reoccurring element I see in most novels today is a small inciting incident or a false start, almost like an action beat before the actual story.

In simple terms, it acts as a prologue without being labeled as such. Does your story have this? If so, how does this help or hinder the rest of your novel?

If your story is a Chosen One prophecy, hit this pronto. If a coming of age tale, express this. Whatever your manuscript is about, find some way to show this as close to the first page. We don't want to dupe the audience; we want genuine fans who devour our novels. Promise them early on and deliver. Once mood and getting to the point are met, now it's time to delve a little deeper, situate the world and characters, and to do this, we slow down a bit.

2. *Whittle, chisel, sculpt*—Write it all, even stuff you won't need if it'll help you as an author, then butcher the hell out of it when editing. If you wrote something that's not necessary, carve it out. If it gives some insight to the plot, character, culture, etc., whittle down to the bare essentials. Use fewer words to get the same meaning across.

This may sound paradoxical when I encourage you to flesh something out though it may not end up in the book. Let me explain. As a general rule, you're correct; I don't waste time if it's not essential. That said, if there's something I'm not wrapping my head around, I'll take a moment to deep dive. Most of the time, this centers around critical choices.

Being a pantser, and not forcing my characters into decisions, they make a choice that I, the author, either don't agree with or question. Most of the time, I think, "This is out of character," and I explore why I thought so. Why out of character? How is it not? At what point did they make this decision, what defining moment? Can I foreshadow this? And once I find that, I center the internal struggle and prose around the defining moment.

Another area in which I explore more is any type of sexual or romantic moment. These elements need to ring with clarity and convey something pivotal. A sex scene should always express character in one form or another through acts, decisions, emotions, body language, etc. If a scene doesn't hit at least one of these elements, you've written titillation, and I'd ask for the necessity.

I write these parts in detail to find those moments, then work backward and focus the scene to the point I wish to express. A final reason why I flesh out endless pages of these scenes is because I want it as well-written as everything else. I don't want to shift the tone in the slightest. I don't want a book with dark, gritty overtures, and the sex scenes resemble *Sesame Street* or *PeeWee's Playhouse*.

So, if there's an element or moment you can't wrap your head around, I encourage you to explore to the fullest extent, insert the crucial aspects, and build to its pinnacle.

3. *Establish one of the following early in the story: physical, cultural, magical, spiritual, or morality (societal mores).* This ties back into rule one. Give the reader something to latch onto and expand. Once they understand your world, they can become a part of it. Give them something to root for or hate. The longer you go without establishing this, the more in limbo they'll feel.

There are many ways to accomplish this from the get-go. If your story opens with an elf, that's a new culture to explore. How many books are written from an elf's perspective? What about a dragon's? Many things can wow your audience, and one is picking the right setting.

When I start an opening chapter, I try to establish the personality right away, especially in the context of their surroundings. Depending on what kind of passage you're writing: a novel, a tome, novella, short story, etc., you may or may not have the leeway to dawdle. In my novella, *The Dark Portal*, I had to introduce the MC, setting, and tone within pages. Almost within paragraphs. Novellas are typically between 30k and 60k words, but if you're writing 60k, you might as well make a novel.

I digress.

Because I chose to hit the novella around the 30k words mark, writing within the confines of a strict word count makes every sentence matter. The atmosphere is introduced from the first paragraph. The MC, at least his initial emotional and mental state, is established at the same time and evolves throughout the story. He's scared, paranoid, anxious ... the tension is riddled within the lines.

4. *Ground your character in a relatable aspect.* I've talked about this at length in an earlier chapter. The categories are money, power, sex, family, knowledge, religion, etc. You can always find more, but these are the most typical or easiest to relate to. Everyone's motivated by something; find your character's motivation, and make it the backbone—it's there, essential, but not the forefront. See rule 3.

Here's something no one thinks about when writing: motivation can change in the story. Sometimes, motivation is altered without being planned; other times, it's intentional. In the movie, *Alien*, Ellen Ripley has a motivational shift in the story, and a good thing, too. Initially, I'd argue Ripley's motivation is money and family. These two incentives—or they can be desires if so inclined—both pull against and reinforce each other, creating internal conflict. She can't take care of her family if she's not getting paid. But this drastically changes to survival. The second half of the movie is all about getting off the moon and ship alive. Utilizing two different motivations and seeing a shift creates tension and a great arc.

5. *Don't control your characters/story, let them go where they need.* Again, this comes from the pantser's/gardener's perspective. Adhering to a rigid outline can stifle creativity. For this reason, when I outline, I mark the tent poles, the significant parts that need to be hit. In between is a journey. When finished with your draft, if you find the plot meandering too much, see rule 2.

Have you ever found yourself introducing a secondary character, but they take over the story? You're faced with two choices, curb them and keep them confined, or let them run wild and free. I'd urge the latter. It can take your story and plot in a whole new direction. You need a protagonist, but why not two? What's wrong with having a cast full of unique and vital characters, all larger than life in their own way? This is where not controlling them comes in.

One thing to keep in mind: you know who the MC is, the other characters don't. Everyone is the MC of their own story. No one sees themselves as the sidekick, just as no real villain deems themselves evil. So, let them live a life of their own, to shine and enhance your story, but when the novel concludes, the MC is apparent to your reader.

6. *Let it sit.* When you finish, put it aside. If it's the first book, go on to craft an outline or flesh out ideas for your next book and beyond. Go start another story. Whatever you do, don't go back into your draft and start the next round. You need to approach with fresh eyes and perspective. Six months would be a reasonable amount of time, long enough for you to be knee-deep in another project. Maybe edit one while writing the other. I've done this as a way to separate the two projects.

Remember: write for you, but edit for your readers. And, like a good wine after opening, let it breathe a little before devouring it.

Seven Types of Conflict

Stories can be broken down into seven types of conflicts. You could argue only six, but making a distinction between gods and supernatural adds an interesting dynamic. This section will be relatively short, but it will get your wheels turning regarding what elements you can add or summarize what your story is about.

Person vs. Self: This struggle is internal. When you give a character two desires that conflict with one another or any type of mental or emotional distress, those elements are drawn from this type. Cinematic representations of this include *Fight Club, Eternal Sunshine of the Spotless Mind*, and *Memento*. Another movie that touches on this and other elements like, person vs. society, is *Joker*.

Person vs. Person: This conflict is the typical storytelling method, and it can be drawn from friends, lovers, antagonists, or any other person in opposition to your lead. Typically, any superhero movie you watch boils down to this type of conflict or *Rocky* for his final bout.

Person vs. Nature: As implied, this is against the elements. *Interstellar* is a superb movie that draws not only from person vs. self and person vs. person but person vs. nature. Think of the black hole. It's a character within the movie, as is time. Don't forget those giant, hundred-foot waves. Leonardo DiCaprio's *Revenant* is another excellent movie about the struggle against nature, as is *127 Hours, Jaws, Twister, Cast Away*, and any world-ending movie.

Person vs. Society: This is a more complex issue to tackle, but the first personification that comes to mind is Orwell's *1984*. Typically, any story where a character rises up against society, government, business, culture, etc., and battles the evil or oppressive construct falls into this definition. *The Scarlet Letter, The Handmaid's Tale*, even *Game of Thrones*, to an extent, are fighting against the societal pressures, norms, or roles.

Person vs. Machine/Technology: The most iconic role and films to date fall in this category: *Terminator 1 & 2*. It also coincides under the next conflict against fate. Another example would be the *Matrix, I, Robot, 2001: A Space Odyssey*, and *Her*.

Person vs. Fate/God(s): As mentioned before, *Terminator*, specifically John and Sarah Connor, fall into this category of fate. *Clash of the Titans*, though pulled from the mythological setting, is a *person vs. god(s)* story.

Person vs. the Supernatural: Almost any paranormal film can be found here, but I also like to add aliens. Another noteworthy entry should be *Lord of the Rings*. If you think about it, *LOTR* has every type of conflict listed above: Frodo's journey standing in for fate, the One Ring for supernatural, Saruman's technology and army breeding, the march of the Ents for nature, the hobbits defying society and going off on an adventure, every battle is vs. person, and Frodo's internal struggle throughout is against himself, which can also be tied back to the supernatural.

There you have the seven types of conflict. So, which does your story incorporate? Is it singular or layered with many different types? Let's move on to a controversial topic: Dialogue tags.

Dialogue Tags

Okay, so this is going to be an opinionated slog to work through on this subject—that's not my opinion I'm referring to, but other peoples'. Without being a jerk and saying all views are invalid, I'm going to say let's put the ego on pause for a moment.

For those who are diehard advocates of "only using said," by the end of this segment, I hope to at least make you waver on your zealotry. For those who run rampant with the strange inserts, I hope you find this constructive. Regardless of which part of the spectrum you sit on, come away with something. With that said, buckle up!

Before delving too deep into the argument at hand, there's something that must be brought up. From what I've seen, the said-only crowd is made up of two groups, the ones who say said-only and leave the disagreement alone, and the other group I dub the caustic touters.

This group is real and vehemently believes that their way is the only one. When looking at the said vs. any other alternative inserted, they mock, ridicule, belittle, and talk down to anyone utilizing anything other than said. They call them amateurs, unprofessional writers, and any other type of slander you can think of. We'll come back to this by the end.

If you are one of these caustic touters, this doesn't help your case. If anything, it turns people off to whatever you have to say, and they'll continue on or double down on their method. Persuading people is about presenting a sound argument—both logical and reasonable. Shaming or delivering the alternative of "if you're not with me, you're the enemy" mentality doesn't help the cause. However, if you're one of those who uses every word except said—and I used to be a part of that group—please continue reading. You need this section.

I know this sounds crazy, but if you are new to the writing community, you'll soon find this is a heavily-contested battleground. I urge each writer, new or otherwise, to see which method works best for you. In this passage, you'll learn there's more to the quarrel than tags. By the end of this section, you'll find the key takeaway, and I hope you incorporate the advice. For those who aren't swayed—on either side of the argument—this segment has merit. Open your eyes to the larger picture. Let's move on.

The purist view: *only* use "said or asked" as they're almost invisible to the reader. Use nothing else. It should be evident in the conversation.

My initial thought is if we are trying to be invisible, let's change the industry to where we put the name at the end of the sentence—character A. The reader can determine how they spoke, letting their imagination run wild. No? Let's obliquely approach this.

As writers, we're describing a world and story. Even with limited world-building, there's detail along the way. We don't just say, "and they reached the building." No, we describe the building, but maybe not in gritty detail. We can say a bakery, bank, workshop, grocery store, or any number of generic descriptors.

Other authors—such as in fantasy—will tell you not only the building but what it's made of, the stone, the wood, the stain or finish on said wood, the door, the hinges or knob on the door, the glass panes, the smell of the place, the carpet—if any, the paint covering the walls, the roof … Had enough? Yet we don't crucify an author when they do this. Why not?

I'm not advocating you should use the most colorful words to describe how a character says something. If you used the same detail here as in everything else, I'd say a substantial revision is needed—stat! But what I'm trying to articulate is the need for leeway when painting a scene for the reader.

Granted, much should be obvious: the way the character is standing, body language, the subject matter itself, personality, the words used; however, adding a few words to show a change in the direction of the conversation shouldn't be rebuked.

Not enough? Let's continue.

If two characters have a shouting match, and one person goes quiet suddenly, there should be no problem showing this. In the example below, let's assume you know the characters are having a heated debate.

> "I told you, I'm not going to do it. I'm not going to apologize for saying what I think."
> "Well, that's why you're going to grow old and die alone! You chase all your friends away because you're a jerk."
> "At this point," he whispered, "I'm not so sure being alone is a bad thing."

Granted, the above isn't an award winner, but the lesson remains: a sudden change, and the dialogue tag signals this. You can also use description to show he's whispering, but now you're using many words to describe one. So, which is better? One word, or a dozen?

"At this point," he said, the anger fading from his face, his words turning brittle, "I'm not so sure being alone is a bad thing."

You decide which is best. Still not compelled? Let's keep going.

Dialogue tags are a part of writing and always will be. There are times when they aren't needed, such as two distinct characters conversing. Action beats can break up the monotony, but along the way, you'll need something more.

To me, writing plays out like a movie, the nuances of the face, and the stressing of a character's words. Everything I've read or opinions from people on the matter have come back with: stick with said. The consensus is employing any other type is the hallmark of an amateur. The "he said, she said" method, in my mind, is tedious, and the author skipped engaging their brain to insert such a trivial word.

Moreover, critics say, "said" almost disappears entirely, and my question would be, "Why use it at all?" The obvious answer is showing who is saying what, but what if we approached other aspects the same way?

What if you wrote a novel with all characters having brown hair and brown eyes? It would be rather one-dimensional and boring, right? What if they all had the same personality? The same goals? Where would be the fun in reading that? Apply this mentality to how they speak.

What if they had the same dialect, the same inflections, the same speech patterns, the same vocabulary? Sounds pretty terrible. The same can be said for the tags—no pun intended—inserted at the beginning, middle, or end of a sentence.

Said is repetitious, and repetition is the killer of anything. Even in the sentence structure. If everything is the same. If all sentences never vary. It can be quite dull. No matter what is said. Always with five-word sentences. Will I still have fans? No one will complain, right? This is the correct way. Always using the same method. Never changing will be awesome. The hallmark of exceptional prose. The five-word sentences suck! It's the same with said. And now, you are bored. But it is okay, right? Because we are staying safe.

This is also how I view 'said,' a sore thumb when repeated with a heavy hand. And yes, you can find published works from best selling authors who do this. And now, you'll say, "Well, end of the argument!"

No.

If I find it repetitious and tedious, many others will, too. I am but one voice; there are hundreds of millions of readers.

Take the dialogue tags below. When you run across a wall of tags in some books, and you've got more than two characters in a conversation, it's monotonous. What if you stumbled onto a passage in a book where this was all you saw?

—*character A said.*

—*B said.*

—*C said.*

—*B said.*

—*A asked.*

—*C said.*

—*B said.*

This isn't inspiring, and yes, I've seen this before. It tells you nothing other than who said what, not how they delivered the words. Yes, there should be other clues such as words, body language, etc., but many books lack those elements in the bigger conversation.

The opposite is true, as well. If you are constantly using different, outlandish tags, it'll be glaring. Implementing numerous adverbs will be as detrimental. Don't use: he postulated, she said magnanimously, he lambasted, she enthused excitedly, he worried greatly—see my point? That'd be terrible, but a sprinkling of alternatives can help paint a vivid picture of how they conversed. You be the judge of what your story needs.

We, as people, don't say things in a bland manner. We don't speak in a monotone voice. We have nuance, stress words, deliver in a constantly-evolving manner based upon emotions or thoughts. Like the five-word sentence, speaking the same way every time is robotic.

For the alternative label crowd, whatever you use should be something direct, articulating what you desire to express, and be as un-intrusive as possible. Save the strange or descriptive words for internal reflections or whatever medium you choose.

In film format, you can distinguish the different deliveries in the scene. You can hear the heartbreak, the anger, the shock, and you can see it, too. Let's not forget the lighting, the swell of music, visual effects, and the sound. All can be noted within seconds, but in novels, you need more than three sentences for the same effect.

This is where utilizing different tags come in. Used correctly with a carefully crafted selection, in addition to the said route and action beats, delivering a blend to catapult your scene shouldn't be a problem.

Humans whisper, they yell, some folks mumble or don't articulate their words, and when they're afraid, their voices change in pitch or tremble. All of this should be taken into account when crafting. Let's not forget much of the spoken word begins on the inside by how someone feels. If afraid, how is their resolve now? Did it crumble away or harden? The inward journey into the character should be reflected in your dialogue, and if you've done your job at defining this moment for them, a tag shouldn't even be necessary.

The **key takeaway** from this section is the blend of said, other tags, action beats, and internal emotions and thoughts. Between the four of these, you should have an ample selection to choose from. To say one of these doesn't exist simply because you don't like it isn't good enough, and that goes for all involved—the said-only crowd, the caustic touters, the crazy label group, and everyone in between.

There's also another group within the fight I haven't mentioned before now. Without saturating the battlefield too much, there's a group that protests no one can speak while laughing or sighing or any other type of expressive use. I disagree. And the notion is easy to disprove.

Take a deep breath like you're going to sigh. As you blow the breath out of your mouth, say, "I need a vacation." Congratulations, you've spoken while sighing. The next time you're in a group and people laugh during the conversation, tune in, and pay attention to whether anyone laughs while speaking. I guarantee there'll be at least one.

One final thought before moving to my last defense: whenever possible, eliminate. Fleshed out characters who speak distinctly in a setting with only two of them, the tags should go at the beginning to show who is saying what. The rest will take care of itself. Not everything spoken needs one, but only insert to draw specific attention to a shift in tone or pace. When possible, cut out as many as you can, but insert when needed.

My last defense is from famous authors. Like the example above where I spoke about some best-selling authors who stick with said, many don't. To only take one at face value and dismiss the other is ludicrous; a different view can flesh out your own ideas far better than you can explore on your own.

For those who are Brandon Sanderson fans, he uses more than said. Granted, he keeps his tag-pool small, and he sticks with basic elements, but he navigates away from the generic. Is he an amateur for doing so? That's the point of contention, right?

And one more for the road. To all *Harry Potter* fans on the said-only bandwagon, Rowling is guilty of using more than said. She loves incorporating different methods of speaking, adverbs in the tag, and a plethora of punctuation to include the exclamation point! Why should this be relevant? I don't know, perhaps she's the world's most famous—and most prosperous—author adored for the *Harry Potter* series when it came out. That should say something about her, right? Is she unprofessional?

There's a lesson here for everyone. Hopefully, this passage has poked enough holes in both sides for you to find the value in the other. Again, it's all a blend.

Do you like the "he said, she said," method or something more diverse? Is using different dialogue tags the mark of an amateur or unprofessional writer? In the end, to each their own. Let's move on.

Writing Dialogue

Did you think we were done? We're not only talking tags but dialogue as a whole, too.

Do you remember Harmon's Circle? The shortened Hero's Journey device? Harmon's Circle fits anywhere in your book, a single scene, an act, the whole book, or a conversation. Without realizing it, for years, I've been doing my own version. Before I begin writing a pivotal scene, I write the tent poles first. I need to hit A, B, and C, then I write. The same can be done with dialogue. Jot your end goal and work your way there.

There's a duality in the advice given to most folks. They say, "Listen to how people talk." This is partially true. Yes, follow that advice, but that's not what ends up on paper. A carved, sculpted, bare-bones version is the final product or should be, with minor exceptions. Let's go over a few guidelines on what to do and not do. These are guidelines because every rule is meant to be broken, and if you find something that works for you, stick with it.

1. Try to avoid one character telling another character how they feel—unless it's one of those scenes. If that person is angry, and his fists are clenched, he's pacing, red-faced, we don't need to hear him tell the other guy, "You piss me off!" This is obvious, and it comes across unrealistic and comical. Instead, have the angry man hurl an insult. "You ^^*(@#$&#()@#!" Now, that's much more like real life.

2. Leave out the long-winded expositions or singular speeches—unless, of course, your character is at a podium and addressing their nation. One thing that bugs

me when reading fantasy authors is when characters stop to have a long speech about their morals, ideals, beliefs, and leaves everyone else awed. Yes, I'm referring to a long series revolving around a sword and the one who wields it.

First, it's quite dull and unrealistic. Keep those moments short, and only use long blocks of dialogue for other settings. Besides, the info dump isn't compelling. And why doesn't anyone ever interject or attack during it? It's like the world went on pause for the rant about how right they are. It's terrible and often motivated by the ideals of the author rather than the character.

3.   Use other elements to convey what words can't express/write it in a subtler manner. Let's say the character sees a therapist, and they want to deal with past trauma. When arriving at the issue, he can't express what happened in words. Now, the therapist can play the guessing game, or your MC can use gestures, facial expressions, or body language to convey. Think about a point in your past where something embarrassing happened to you, and you've never told anyone. Think about how you'd convey that to someone without saying the details outright. How would that sound? That's what I'm getting at.

4.   Cut all small talk—this is filler, uninteresting, and makes the reader dislike you. And this goes back to what I was saying earlier about listening to real conversations. In real-world interactions, people have small talk, pleasantries. In books, you don't follow this rule. You cut this. In fact, it doesn't exist. Ever. And this is a practiced duality.

5.   Names in dialogue. This is also a rule often bent when needed. When speaking to your friend or parent, you don't usually say their name. Yes, in the beginning, to get their attention, but often later in the conversation, you don't. If utilizing names, use sparingly. Further, if you have a group of people talking in your book, and your

MC addresses a new person, it's okay to use their name in this regard. Between two, though, it's not necessary. Use with caution.

6. Characters with similar voices: Make sure each of your characters sounds unique. Does one of them say a particular phrase a lot? This shows the uniqueness when no dialogue tag is present.

Remember: if you can cut tags and still make clear who's talking, do it. This is one of those ways. Within the differences of vocabulary and tone, you can make characters shine with quirkiness, humor, sarcasm, or accents—though I recommend going easy on the last one. Sure, accents are important, but if every time they talk, the reader has to pause and figure out what they are trying to say, it's a detriment. So, tone it down enough to get the point across. And if the accented person is your MC, just know you'll have to do this in every line of dialogue, and it's easy to forget your accent rules, so write them down.

7. Repeating what we know. If you've said it once, there's no need to repeat five more times. Once is enough. Twice if it's a new chapter after a long break, and you're reminding the reader. If your MC says, "Quick, we must head to the bank to stop the robber." Don't later say, "We've got to get to the bank—hurry!" But you could say, as they're hurrying, "The bank is up ahead." Why is this okay? We don't know how far the bank is, only that you're going. Is it one block over? Across town? In a different city? This information needs to be made clear.

8. Make the conversations advance the plot. If what they're talking about isn't pushing the main point, then it needs to reveal something about the character, advance a side plot, build romance/friendship, or some other type of revelation. If your dialogue isn't doing any of these, it's time to cut. Kill your darlings.

9. If your character and the reader know what came before (backstory), don't hash it again in dialogue. This is one of those points when telling the reader is better than showing. If your MC knows something detailed and long-winded, and they meet a new character, it's better to summarize this exchange with a sentence or two.

I'm sure there are more instances anyone could find, but this is a strong base in which to start. Go through each of these guiding points and through your manuscript. Did you find a place where you might've faltered? This can be quick fixes, but if your novel is replete with the same mistakes, you've got your work cut out. Let's move on.

Action

Writing action may be one of the most challenging parts for writers, not because they can't convey it, but because of a pacing issue or lack of tension. Another factor, if you think in terms of cinema, is how close or far the action is, and I don't mean a car chase. When two people sit and talk, the story might be progressing, but they're static.

Let's take a few examples from the silver screen to help articulate. *Transformers.* I'm not going to rip on it in terms of storytelling—we're talking about action. There's a lot in those movies. You've got giant robots shifting right before your eyes, some about twelve feet tall, others can take up an entire city block. The maxim for *Transformer* movies is "the bigger, the better," and in writing, this isn't often the case.

But in terms of their fight scenes, how close they are to the camera, sometimes you can't tell what you're looking at. It happens so fast, so close, that it just registers as movement. If this is an approach you want to take with two characters dueling, you might get away with it. However, writing such scenes can bog down the pace with too much technicality your audience may know nothing about.

Now, let's talk about *Lord of the Rings: The Two Towers.* Do you recall the scene when Gandalf leads the charge down the mountainside into the horde of ten thousand? That far off view works quite well in that setting, giving you a distant view at the two sides, their numbers, and movement on the battlefield, a superb method for setting the stage for your conflict if you have armies duking it out. If the whole battle is written in such a manner, it may not come across as tense.

Since we're on *LOTR*, let's hop over to *The Return of the King.* At the end, we see our heroes surrounded by uncounted legions outside the Black Gate. Aragorn leads the charge, and the battle ensues. In this scene, there's less of a wide shot and more within the ranks. We watch Aragorn's, Legolas's, Gimli's, and Gandalf's personal battles within the larger construct, which gives pacing to the overall struggle. In fact, I dare say all the fighting in the *LOTR* trilogy is superb.

So, what am I saying? There are lessons to be learned with these examples, what to do and what not to do.

The word action is broad and can cover many aspects, but when you think about the word, you tend to remember movies and fight scenes—superheroes flying around and crashing into things, or destroying buildings. Even cinematography has changed to compensate for the faster beats in film. Take fight scenes from old Bruce Lee movies or the original trilogy of *Star Wars* and compare them to Marvel, DC, or *Taken* movies. The cuts are quick and give a choppy feeling infused with nitrous oxide.

How do we translate this to the novel, to show a fight's quickness, a chase, a moment without coming off as cliche? Cliches hurt a story as much as underwriting a scene. What are some examples of cliched, quick writing?

As quick/fast as lightning…
Within a heartbeat…
Time slowed…

Cliches are not the most terrible thing to use when emphasizing something specific, though I'd caution using 'it's raining cats and dogs' unless literally doing so. How does this pertain to the action beats? Well, if time slowed, I'd hope whoever is slowing time has the power to do so. Can you express the same thing using another manner? Maybe heightened reflexes or senses?

An important note: don't hinge the success of the entire scene by getting too hung up on cliches within the first draft. Leave them. Move on and write the scene. Worry about your cliches in the revision and editing phases. Also, be wary of the ones that don't seem like cliches.

Moving past this sore point, our goal is to express what's happening. What makes an action beat? Is it driving a car? Driving isn't action-driven, but it *is* an action. What about a sword fight or a battle with magic? Ah, there's our seam: the clang of steel ringing with magic whooshing overhead in a glittering yet caustic stream. Our characters are in mortal peril, but if your reader doesn't think so, there's a problem.

So, we know what we want and how the movements play out in our heads, but how to write it down? A gross oversimplification is to use shorter sentences. Have you ever read a novel filled with too many short or long sentences? It makes the book either feel sporadic and jarring or convoluted and drawn out. Varying sentence length is crucial to the success of your scenes, but in fast-paced execution, we want to focus on the shorter sentences broken up by a few longer ones.

A distinction must be made here: you can use longer sentences in this approach, and if broken by correct comma usage, you can read clearly and keep your pacing. Do you recall that earlier segment of dialogue tags when I had a whole paragraph with five-word sentences? We don't want that. Vary your sentence length, favoring the shorter side.

Another element bogging down the writing is the vernacular phrasing or over-the-top flowery language. We want our sentences short and concise, specific, but we also want the reader to understand the most fundamental elements. In a sword fight, your reader might not understand what a riposte is, but you can educate them.

He executed a riposte, countering on the heels of the villain's attack.

This is a method I use, letting the reader digest the correct terminology while breaking down the layman's terms. The next time they see riposte, they'll know. It's okay to use the tell method every once in a while, but overabundant technicalities can kill. Not everyone is a fencing expert.

While swords may loop overhead and spells are cast with an intricate weaving of the wand, don't lose momentum by focusing on this aspect. Another element that will ground your writing into something visceral is the emotional aspect and physical strain. Does your character suffer from a necessity to kill? Chances are, they don't. Killing another human, an act far from natural, should bear heavy mental and emotional toll on your character.

Storytime: In a sequel I'm working on in my main fantasy series, an assassin took on an apprentice. The apprentice threw herself into the training, the physicality, the fighting, and joint manipulation, but throughout the entire novel, she doubted she'd be able to kill anyone.

At the climax of the story, she faced a situation to kill or be killed, and she chose to save her own life. While some may consider this method a copout, the decision defined by her internal struggle honed her arc—going from someone who vowed to never kill no matter the circumstance, to killing to save herself. What emotional hurdle does your character face? What drove them to this point? Are the consequences still warring within them?

Another vital element is the dialogue in a fight scene. This can kill all momentum if not done well. Don't rely on this point in the story to have the villain deliver a long-winded diatribe, or let the hero make a grand speech on truth, justice, and the righteousness of their quest. I won't say the reader doesn't care at this point, but the culmination, the payoff to the story you started, needs to be the focus.

Let's take a gander at a few movies where the dialogue was superb before the action scene.

> Avengers: *Age of Ultron*
> Ultron: "I'm glad you asked that because I wanted to take this time to explain my evil plan." *Immediately attacks.*
>
> *SW: ESB*: Darth Vader and Luke at Cloud City
> DV: "You've learned much, young one."
> LS: "You'll find I'm full of surprises."
> *Boom, right back to the fight.*
>
> *The Dark Knight*: Joker and Batman, final fight.
> Joker: "Ah, you made it. I'm so thrilled."
> Batman: "Where's the detonator?"
> Joker: "Go get him!" *Dogs attack.*

These short examples are a way to up the conflict in a scene. All of these are short—what's the point of these moments? To articulate and define which side they're landing on. A quick recount of the stakes ratchets the tension beforehand.

I use dialogue in my action scenes, but sparingly. This ups the stakes as the hero and villain come to blows. But you can also use an exchange to slow the scene down to a pivotal moment. Again, they aren't supposed to be long-winded, but should be longer and more poignant. Let's take a look at a few moments when dialogue was done right during an action beat that slowed down the scene.

Avengers: Infinity War: Thanos to Tony Stark.
> Thanos: "You have my respect, Stark. When I'm done, half of humanity will still be alive. I hope they remember you."
>
> Wow, he defeated Iron Man and company, and Tony realizes there's nothing he can do to stop Thanos. Further, Thanos is articulating the stakes again, and the threat of "I hope they remember you," is a nice, weighty finality.

SW: ROTJ: Darth Vader vs. Luke Skywalker on the Death Star.
> LS: "Your thoughts betray you, Father. I feel the good in you, the conflict."
> DV: "There is no conflict."
> LS: "You couldn't bring yourself to kill me before, and I don't believe you'll destroy me now."
> DV: "You underestimate the power of the dark side. If you will not fight, then you will meet your destiny." *Throws lightsaber.*

For this next one, let's explore some different beats.

> *LOTR: The Return of the King*: Sam and Frodo in Mt. Doom
> Sam: "Give me your hand." *Pause.* "Take my hand."
> Frodo: Looks down at the lava.
> Sam: "Don't you let go." *Pause.* "Don't let go. Reach!"
> Frodo: Clasps his hand, and they run out as the mountain begins to erupt.

What I like about the last example is that this takes place in the lull between two separate scenes, the fight over the ring and escaping. This is a crucial moment when Frodo makes a critical choice to live. I went into the movies knowing about the books, but I had never read them. I thought Frodo would let go. Had it been my book, I would've leaned towards this decision. Even though there's a wholesome-esque ending to the trilogy, it's still bittersweet. As for the cinematic portrayal, it's quite a satisfying conclusion to the story.

Action, like dialogue, is more than words on the page. There is action, pace, emotional and physical struggle, tension, and sentence variation. It's hard to recollect all this in the moment, but that's why we go through revisions. Like many sections within this book, this portion is brushing the surface with broad strokes, but these sweeping points will go a long way to helping you craft excellent prose.

The only thing you should worry about in the first draft is getting it down on paper. Excellent writing comes with the revisions. Nothing is perfect on the first try. Let your beta readers and critiquers hone your scenes as needed.

Remember: make sure your writing is top quality before doling out.

Risking the Characters

Exposing characters to risk can bring added value to the attachments the reader has made to your protagonist. Risk makes life exciting and frustrating. Whether it's heartache, the thrill of gambling, or everyday tasks, it's inherent—though the latter is negligible. When you get in the car to go grocery shopping, you gamble against the likelihood of getting into a motor vehicle accident. But how does this translate to your character?

Most books are about a journey like Frodo in *Lord of the Rings*. Two movies or shows come to mind. The first is *The Empire Strikes Back*. Luke fought at the Battle of Hoth, but you were pretty sure he would survive. How about when he rushes off to face Vader? You might've thought he's still safe, except for the dark warning Yoda gave Obi-Wan as Luke launches into the sky.

When Yoda's face glows from the light of the X-wing's engines, Kenobi says, "That boy is our last hope." To which Yoda utters the terrible line, "No, there is another. Now, matters are worse." What George Lucas did with those two simple lines makes the viewer go, "Oh, crap, Luke's in trouble!" Granted, this is a PG version of jeopardy, but it still hits the mark with kids and first-time viewers.

A noteworthy entry is by another man named George. The book series and TV show, *Game of Thrones*, introduced mortal peril to our favorite fellows. The pilot episode sets the tone for the entire series with a boy pushed from a tower. Bran lived but was crippled for life. Not only that, but halfway through the first season, Ned Stark is wounded in combat, and Daenerys's brother is given a golden crown fit for a king. Then, they kill off the protagonist for the first season, Ned Stark. These simple yet effective injuries and deaths set the mood for the whole show, and the viewer knows no one is safe.

This is the risk I'm talking about. Most folks in their stories have plot armor, whether visible or not. When's the last time you read a book where the protagonist is killed off in the first third of the book? When I watched *Game of Thrones*, that was my introduction to Westeros, and I didn't think they'd go through with killing Ned. God, was I wrong.

So, let's start with the adage "Kill your darlings." In this context, we aren't discussing passages in your writing that mean a lot to you, but specifically your characters. I'm not advocating to kill them all, though you certainly may. Actually, that would be an interesting twist. Your characters need to suffer to grow.

Think of a bad time in your life, one that brought you to your lowest point. How did you come out after this? Are you better, stronger, wiser for it? Back to your character, did they suffer emotionally? Did someone they care for spurn them? Did they lose a family member? What about mental or physical? Are they training in extreme and harsh environments? Did they suffer a nervous breakdown? Physical suffering can manifest from a plethora of incidents. Did they lose an arm? Perhaps they were captured and turned into a slave? Were they starved?

These aspects are the turning points for your character. They need to face crisis and adversity. How did they overcome it? Perhaps they never did, not entirely, which would be an excellent way for the problem to linger throughout a series. A unique way to let doubt enter your reader's mind is to put your character into a near-impossible situation. They can overcome it with cunning, brute strength, patience, but mayhaps your lead doesn't possess those aspects. Can the impulsive soldier sit by and wait? Can the weak man defeat an adversary of immense strength? Just don't let them get away unscathed.

What are some other ways you can add risk to the individuals of your story? How do we ratchet up the tension? More often than not, if you can play to real elements or historical origins—such as the superstition of witchcraft—it gives your story more weight, especially in the proper setting. While plot and character are critical aspects of your story, let us not forget this marvelous part, which lends credibility to other elements of your book.

Sex

How are oxygen and sex similar? Both are no big deal unless you're not getting any.

Welcome to the most controversial topic we'll discuss. If you have no intention of including this in your book, skip this section. For those of you who are curious or sold on writing this element, stick around.

Sex sells. Whether people admit it or not, they want it in some capacity. Some see it as light and fun; others treat it as something sacred and profound—but can it not be both?

For readers, unless it's romance or erotica—and those are two very different genres—there almost always needs to be a reason beyond horniness. In real life, if you're in the mood, you and your partner can knock boots, but in the book world, it needs to be more, especially the first time.

Sex without revealing character is what the audience refers to as titillation. Erotica is different. We know why we're reading. We want the thrashing between the sheets. However, in other genres, this is approached differently. If you're going to write a scene between two well-established characters down the road, there is no problem.

That said, don't drag this out. Don't wait for four of five books to take the next step—only to fade to black. The longer the tease, the more of a romp you need. The payoff needs to be worth the wait. Your readers have been reading this sexual tension, this rise to climax (for lack of a better word) in their relationship. Don't cheat them. The unfolding scene can tell a reader much about their personalities as any conversation, action beat, or narrative passage—perhaps more.

Most of the time—though not always—you can tell who wrote a scene, a male or female author. Small tells give it away. The perfect scene would be written in a manner where the reader cannot discern who wrote the scene. Male authors tend to focus on visual aspects because men are visual and physical creatures. They also focus on how something feels or how they are touched, the physical pleasure.

Female authors tend to be more in touch with the other senses, smells, and emotions. A female friend—also a writer—once told me women want sensory overload to escape their heads. This insight is invaluable. Without dragging this out like the build-up to a prominent scene, we will jump right in.

General Rule of Thumb: "If sex can reveal character, advance the plot, or increase tension—and the genre allows, encourages, or permits it—then the writer should *consider* including it in the novel." At least, that's the premise of all the advice I've read or seen over the years.

1: There's no right or wrong way to write sex ... in your first draft.

Writing about the age-old rhythm is about the revision—the added layers and textures—not the bare bones or the deed itself. Your first draft needs to be rough, dirty, and read almost like you're watching adult entertainment. The point is to get it down on paper, block out the movements/positions, and the culmination.

Don't edit when you are writing your first scene. Don't interrupt the flow. Don't get up from your computer!

If you cannot sit down and write out a scene without interruption or getting up, don't start.

Your first draft should make you cringe. Use every foul word and modern term you need.

2: If you're not turned on—at least on some level—by what you're writing, your reader isn't either. It's not immersive, and that means they're not engaged or committed.

This reinforces the first point. However, authors tend to inject their own preferences, biases, or prejudices into their works, and sex is no different. If you're going to write about something without experience, you must: A) do your homework, and B) edit out your own preferences— whether it's liking, loving, or hating.

If your character is supposed to love BDSM, but you don't, it'll show in your writing. If the sexual act is something you hate, it'll be clear in the text.

3: There are many different types of sex (kinks) and scenes. Can you name a few? If not, use the list below.

Romance, erotica, love scenes, first-time excursion (virginal), forbidden fruit notion/mentality, reconnection, casual, fantasy-fulfillment...

Point three reinforces the previous point. Know your character, know your scene. Sex isn't perfect, as in movies, which are meant to arouse and be artful.

Sex can be funny, odd, tense, or evoke anxiety. It can set or shift the tone of your novel. It's not always about gratification and the climax.

4: The act is about love and/or gratification; reading the scene is about the senses —to engage the reader.

How can sex be used to engage the reader other than the act? It can reveal anatomical differences between species (elves, trolls, werewolves, etc.), reference historical context, or express character and spur development.

5: Guys are visual creatures, and will write more about how a woman looks and feels than anything else.

While this is great for a male audience, it can be a turn off for others. Men and women both view sex and write it differently. In the deed, details are phenomenal—but it's the delivery that makes or breaks a scene. Guys, don't fixate on describing breasts the whole time. Ladies, don't skim over or skip visual or physical details that stimulate half your audience.

6: Sex in first-person POV can engage half your audience and alienate the other half…

Choose wisely when writing. Consider this early—during your planning or outlining phase.

Word Choice—Mood killers:

What kills your mood? Headaches and body aches? Sickness? Fatigue? Here are a few others: derogatory statements, repugnant stench, obnoxious behavior, bad hygiene.

There are mood killers in novel-sex too—but they come from word choice. Steer clear unless intentional. Words that turn readers off include (but are not limited to) clinical or medical terms: penis, vagina, erection, phallus, or any iteration.

Derogatory and vulgar words like cock, pussy, vag, dick, taint, boner, and tits don't help your cause either.

Comical terms or slang should also be avoided at all costs: yodeling in the gully, fun bags, choking the chicken, beating the bishop, love pillows, tallywacker, daisy chain, jerk the gurgan, the one-eyed wonder worm, rod of love, cotton pony, Roman candlestick, and purple-headed yogurt slinger. If any of these or others are listed in your writing, for the love of everything holy, take them out.

Everyday Terms: If there's a modern term for an activity, don't use it— unless it's in dialogue or summary. Even then, use it sparingly. Take with a grain of salt. Rules are meant to be broken, and I can guarantee someone has already used the above.

Another thing to consider is prose: you don't want overly flowery language, yet poetic sentences can work if used in moderation. However, don't lose your audience in allegories or obscure means to describe what's happening.

> **Storytime**: I once read a novel in college, and no, I don't remember the name, but I didn't realize the characters had sex because of the saturated prose. I honestly thought they were drunk or in an altered mental state.

Word Choice—Words You Can Use: Not everyone will agree, and you can't please everyone—but here are common words I've seen used across genres.

> Men: *shaft, length, arousal, firmness, hardness, manhood, member, tip, rod, staff.*
> Women: *core, sheath, sex, heat, wetness, flower, bud, globes, mounds, contours.*
> Both: *Peak, backside, bottom, butt, rear, rear end, rump.*

Repetition: the monotonous, boring side of writing sex.

Repetition will kill a scene and a book. If you're using the same word or phrase of words, this kills all steam and momentum you are building.

> **Storytime:** I once read a book with well-written escapades, but they used cock in almost every sentence while giving the girl's anatomy a plethora of words, and some of which I've never heard before. First, it was the wrong word and threw me out of the scene every time. The repetition drove me insane.

The same can be said of actions within the scene. This is the best time to break out your thesaurus and think of new ways to describe body parts, motions, emotions, dialogue tags, and senses.

Taking two movements and describing them in different ways: I'm not advocating all these, but here are some examples. Some are questionable, some usable. I've seen most in mainstream books.

> Men: *breach, burrow, bury, dart, delve, dip (into), embed, enter, fill, impale, insert, penetrate, pierce, plunge (into), press (down on or into), probe, prod, push, ravage, settle (between/into), sheath, shove, sink (into), spear, stab, thrust, tunnel.*

> Women: *anchor, bear (down on), cover, grind, rock (against), rotate, settle over (mouth or body), spread, straddle, surround, tangle/entangle, twine/entwine, sinking into someone/sliding down onto, riding tightened thighs, pulling hips down.*

Detail: Is there such a thing as too much? Detail is a staple in fantasy: learning about a new world, the magic system, its currency, customs and cultures, rites, religions, beliefs, and politics. However, once you bring sex into the mix, well, people tend to get cagey and turn away. Like it or not, American culture shuns sexuality. A prime example is the *Fifty Shades of Grey* rating. What we gave an R or NC-17 rating received the equivalent of a PG-13 or lower around the world.

George R. R. Martin, the author of *Game of Thrones*, said,

> *"I can describe an axe entering a human skull in great explicit detail, and no one will blink twice at it. I provide a similar description, just as detailed, of a penis entering a vagina, and I get letters about it and people swearing off. To my mind, this is kind of frustrating—it's madness. Ultimately, in the history of [the] world, penises entering vaginas have given a lot of people a lot of pleasure; axes entering skulls, well, not so much."*

And he makes a valid point. Look at Hollywood and what's considered a good or bad movie. Take *John Wick*, for example. Most people love these films, myself included, and there's violence galore. Had there been as much sex as bullets boring through heads in gritty detail, it would've bombed at the box office. Why?

When George R. R. Martin was asked if he has too much gratuitous sex and details, he responded,

> "Well, I'm not writing about contemporary sex—it's medieval. There's a more general question here that doesn't just affect sex or rape, and that's this whole issue of what is gratuitous? What should be depicted? I have gotten letters over the years from readers who don't like the sex, they say it's " gratuitous." I think that word gets thrown around and what it seems to mean is "I didn't like it." This person didn't want to read it, so it's gratuitous to that person.
>
> And if I'm guilty of having gratuitous sex, then I'm also guilty of having gratuitous violence, and gratuitous feasting, and gratuitous description of clothes, and gratuitous heraldry, because very little of this is necessary to advance the plot. But my philosophy is that plot advancement is not what the experience of reading fiction is about. If all we care about is advancing the plot, why read novels? We can just read CliffsNotes.
>
> "A novel, for me, is an immersive experience where I feel as if I have lived it, and that I've tasted the food, and experienced the sex, and experienced the terror of battle. So, I want all of the detail, all of the sensory things—whether it's a good experience or a bad experience, I want to put the reader through it. To that mind, detail is necessary, showing not telling is necessary, and nothing is gratuitous."

Detail Continued: Sex can spice up your novel—make your reader focus, engage them, ensnare—but too much can make them bored, roll their eyes, skim, skip, or just quit reading. Adding this element can also change the plot and character motivations. What about the guy who is infatuated with the girl, but she takes another man to bed? Is this plot advancement? How will this act change the character dynamic? Is there another antagonist for our MC?

Author Laurel K. Hamilton once spent thirty pages (might be an exaggeration) on sensory overload while her character thought about, fantasized, envisioned, daydreamed, and debated taking someone she had just met to bed. The character did in the end, and the scene was about three pages. In many ways, the lead up was far more detailed than the act itself, and the payoff didn't live up to the tantalizing of the character before the engagement.

Best advice: let the scene grow as big or shrink as little as you want. Worry about adding to or editing the length after a few rewrites. A tasty two-page romp with adequate detail to understand what's going on may be preferable to many readers than a twenty-page Olympian experience. A sizzling four-page with those same details but establishes facets of your character is even better. Neither size nor detail by themselves equates to spectacular or atrocious scenes.

The 5 Senses: Guys are about visual and touch/physical gratification. Most of the time, though not always, you can tell where a male or female author wrote it. The perfect scene would make it indiscernible who wrote it.

Male Focus: Guys will focus on what drives them—what they can see and touch is what matters. Those details tend to focus on breasts, ass, face, waist, maybe hair, and eyes. The only sensations guys tend to notice is the throbbing in their pants, the build-up of blood, and the sting/itch/ yearn to release. Though perfume is something they'll remember, too.

Women writing men need to take these details into account. Men express their feelings and love (and receive love) through the deed more than words and actions. Guys writing guys need to mention these details without fixating on them. Focus on everything but this.

Preferences: To Be or Not To Be Vanilla.

Don't shy away from intercourse that's not "your" type—there's more to fornication than this or vanilla preferences.

Remember: it's not about your choices, your tastes, your desires, but your character's. What may not be for you doesn't mean it stops existing.

However, the key takeaway: **DON'T FEEL OBLIGATED** because someone pressures you into writing something. You're under no obligation to appease anyone. In the end, it's your novel, your story, and you decide. If you want to write sex scenes, but not about male on male or female on female, then don't. If you don't want any at all, don't put it in. You, the author, answer to no one, and that's the end of the argument.

Remember: A sex scene doesn't necessarily mean vaginal intercourse must occur; other forms and variants may qualify. Foreplay—if you don't categorize this the same as the main event—and teasing can be grouped in here.

Other sexual preferences: The mild to the downright bizarre, all exist in the world, and therefore, should theoretically exist in your world. If you don't have a character with a specific preference or not in an expressed POV, I don't think there's a need to bring it up. It's like my world-building method, no sense in deep diving something that won't end up in the book.

The list includes, but is not limited to: pinching, spanking, hair pulling, tying up, biting, scratching, anal, blindfolding, group, swingers, two-on-one, threesomes, polyamory, BDSM (Bondage Discipline/ Domination Submission And Masochism), play-acting scenarios, fantasy/ wish fulfillment, body suspension fetish, choker/collar fetish, harness restraint, pleather, it's near endless.

Dialogue Tags: How To Say Something During Intimacy.

For those who hate any dialogue tag other than *said*, this is the moment to put your hang-up in timeout. *Said* will not add to the flavor you weave in the scene. Use alternatives to enhance the sensual nature: purred, cooed, whispered, breathed, whimpered, teased. This also reinforces the argument from earlier that people don't always speak generically.

There's a lot more than what we've covered, but this is a solid starting point—a guideline to help you craft your next enticing scene. Personally, I agonize over these scenes more than any other. I want them well-written with the right amount of detail. However, I do write subtly, too, and the reader can fill in many blanks. If I rewrote my book five times before sending it to my editor, I feasibly doubled or tripled the writing and editing of these scenes.

Let's take a gander at skippable moments.

What Readers Skip

This segment won't be all-encompassing, and it will be rather light, more because it's straightforward and self-explanatory.

Info dumps kill all momentum in a story and are somewhat lazy writing. Not every info dump is, but most tend to be. Moreover, it usually falls under telling rather than showing.

Back story and flashbacks. These are great for revealing character, but too many will make the reader question why you have the majority of the novel jumping into the past rather than staying in the present. The back story should be sprinkled sparingly. Don't write about it unless pertinent. However, some books run parallel timelines within their novels to show a younger version of the character and how they evolved into the MC. Brandon Sanderson's *Stormlight Archive* comes to mind.

Research. Too much science mumbo jumbo or info-dumping in this category bogs down the progress. When you're writing about horses or saddles or swords, give your character enough information to show the reader you did your research, but not enough to bore us. If it's too long-winded, readers will skip. One section I skipped is in *Brisingr* when Eragon forged his sword. I know many who loved this segment. I didn't. Or suppose it's science fiction, and your scientist character goes off the deep end with a vocabulary and abstract theories that doctors or chemical engineers struggle to understand. In that case, you need to dial it back.

Too much detail. Do you recall what I said earlier in the book? Sacrifice the lengthy prose on the altar of precision? Give us enough detail to see the world around us or the person in front of us, but we don't need the life journey of the timber in each building, or a detailed slog of someone's facial pores. Unless, of course, you're writing a character that's hyper-aware of such things.

Jargon, accents, and foreign words. Each region or culture in your world should have unique words, languages, and jargon, but if it's the only thing they use while speaking, it'll come across as unbearable. Accents are hit and miss. If the character speaks with a heavy accent, and you use apostrophes to show the missing sounds, but that's all their dialogue, your audience may hate you.

Summaries of previous novels. If you are in the third book of a series or trilogy, you need to use small moments to refresh past events, so your reader is caught up. However, these should be succinct. Don't detail it in pages. Summarize. Yes, in this instance, it's okay to use telling.

Cliched storytelling. Waking up from a dream or in the morning is a staple of cliched entries. We don't need to know how they prepared for the day. Daydreaming and mirror staring as a means of revealing the character to the reader, phrases like "little did he know," and blaming atrocious behavior of characters on upbringing or other external forces is also weak and cliched storytelling.

Connecting dots. Don't spell out everything for your reader. Give them some credit to make the connections. Unless, of course, you have so many plot twists that it's a must.

Okay, that's a shortlist. I'm sure there's more, but these are the big ones. On to the next section.

Interludes, Prologues, Epilogues, & Epigraphs

Let's talk about some of my favorite things. Like my aversion to simple and repetitive dialogue tags, my opinion on this topic is in the minority. Perhaps I'm a little old fashioned. That said, for the most part, I love IPEE, or interludes, prologues, epilogues, and epigraphs.

Let's start with my negative: interludes. I'm not a fan. I understand the intent, a pause from your normal viewing pleasure, but if you're going to write an interlude, and the character will appear more than once, write them in as a chapter. I don't want a disruption from the story once it's started. Keep the chapters coming with the characters I adore.

Still, interludes can be a great way to introduce new characters who might crop up later in the book or in the next one. If this latter is the case, is there any way to save the character's entry for the next book? Perhaps start the next entry with them. I had a character in my first book that I removed and placed in the second because he didn't fit into the overall story. Introducing him in the second novel in chapter one gave him a greater emphasis, and the reader is less likely to dismiss him.

Lastly, on interludes, there are some exceptions. In *The Kingkiller Chronicles*, Patrick Rothfuss does something I haven't seen before. Again, I'm not a voracious reader like most folks. The interludes are used to bring the story from the narration of first person past to the third person present narration. It's still the same character but two distinct moments in time. The switch in narration perspective also helps emphasize this, and it's a way to split up the novel and pacing. Where do you stand on interludes? Love them or hate them?

Let's move on to prologues. Let the groaning begin. Don't get me wrong, some prologues are terrible, but not all. Most start cliched: a dream, someone dies at the end, it's about some distant past event, it's something "cool" but with no impact on the story, etc. This happens more than you think, which is why so many people skip them.

My philosophy is a prologue should be like a resume, no longer than two pages, because people won't read them. That's it, super simple. You can capture the reader with something short and to the point. I like in medias res, to start in the middle. That, in a nutshell, is my prologue, a brief glimpse into the story.

So, do I skip prologues when I read? You bet. If it's longer than five pages, I'll skip unless it's an audible book on 1.5x to 1.75x speed. I'm one of those who doesn't like to jump to the end of a section, but I will for a prologue. If someone dies at the end, or they wake up, or you realize it's a memory, I jump to chapter one. Not all prologues are bad, but not all are good either. It's a personal preference. If someone told me to cut it, the only thing I would do is label it chapter one, because it's that important. I don't waste time when writing. If it's garbage or useless, I cut it out on my own.

Epilogues hold a special place in my heart. When the tale closes, the main parts are covered, but you may not fully resolve it. This is where epilogues come in. Think of it this way, in some regards, epilogues are those credit scenes at the end of a movie. All you Marvel fans know what I'm talking about. Almost everyone loves them despite sitting through fifteen minutes of white text on a black screen. Hopefully, the music is decent and composed by Hans Zimmer.

For me, epilogues tease what will come, or it gives a more robust resolution to the story. In many ways, the conclusion arrives in the last chapter, answering all those significant questions, or leaving it wide open for the sequel. While not directly impacting the story, the epilogue can have an enormous effect on the development to come. Again, it's anticipatory.

Some of you may be wondering what an epigraph is. It's a short saying, inscription, or quotation that represents a theme. I'm enamored with this because not every idea is simple. For the *Spider-Man* movies, you have something that has become so cliched by now: 'with great power comes great responsibility.' Take another superhero movie like *The Dark Knight*. You could say the motif of 'some men just wanna watch the world burn' or 'everything burns' could be the epigraph, but I would argue Harvey Dent's passage would be the epigraph. "You either die a hero, or you live long enough to see yourself become the villain." This simple sentence conveys a profound thought.

Epigraphs are a way for you to express your novel's premise in the way you intend. Books can have a single theme or multiple. Also, some themes are open to interpretation, something perhaps unintended as an author.

In one of my stories, I chose: "The things we aspire to be are the things that cause us to fail." It's more complicated than 'absolute power corrupts absolutely' or 'love conquers all.' While it can be interpreted as 'absolute power corrupts absolutely,' my epigraph remains *true* to the original premise.

The epigraph reveals the depth of thought that transcends the novel. What if the epigraph for the next book you read was a famous JFK quote? "Ask not what your country can do for you—ask what you can do for your country." What tone does this set for the overall novel?

What do you think? Do you hate epigraphs, epilogues, and prologues? How do you determine what you skip over? Are you a cloistered old-fashioned reader, or do you want chapter one and only the last chapter?

It's something to think about when determining your style.

The First Chapter Emphasis

The first chapter emphasis, and by association, the first line, are hyped up a lot. You'll hear a lot of people say, "You've got to snare the reader in the first line!" Yes, there's an element of truth to that, but such scrutiny will likely get you too worked up to see the bigger picture. Your first sentence needs to be enticing, yes, but it's not the end-all, be-all.

How many people do you know read the first sentence of a book and say, "Well, that sucked," and then put the book down? I've never met a single soul who confesses to this.

Let's take a glance at a few first lines from some books.

In Brandon Sanderson's *Mistborn*, the first line in the prologue-excluding the epigraph at the top is:

"Ash fell from the sky."

It paints a picture, no doubt; short and simple, it could be volcanic ash, a forest burning, or from a chimney. We don't know, but we got an idea of what we're looking at. But is this mind-blowing? No.

How about Jacqueline Carey's *Kushiel's Dart*?

> "Lest anyone should suppose that I am a cuckoo's child, got on the wrong side of the blanket by lusty peasant stock and sold into indenture in a short-fallen season, I may say that I am House-born and reared in the Night Court proper, for all the good it did me."

The prose is immaculate, almost poetic. Perhaps a touch flowery, but well-written. At the least, it's an exciting premise, but long. What does this and *Mistborn* have in common? Both are intriguing. What is dissimilar? Long vs. short, the prose, and one paints the environment while the other begins with internal character monologue.

Let's look at the first book in one of my favorite trilogies from Mercedes Lackey and James Mallory, *The Outstretched Shadow*.

> "The garden market positively thronged
> with people, clustered around the wagons
> just in from the countryside."

Good locale set up with a vivid atmosphere of the populace, but not earth-shatteringly awesome.

And one more for the road, *The Name of the Wind* by Patrick Rothfuss. The prologue:

> "It was night again."

This sets up the time of day, and it's shorter than Brandon's.

What do all these first sentences have in common? None of them are fantastic, at least in the sense that everyone emphasizes—and that's the point I'm making. The first sentence is overrated. They will not break your book. Objective completed, let's move on.

Now, let's talk about the importance of the first chapter. Yes, I can see folks putting down the book after the first one. I'm guilty of that, but that's the kind of reader I am. You've got a chapter to at least ensnare my attention. If you haven't done so by the novel's premise, the characters, or the prose, I won't continue reading. If the author passes the test, I give them five chapters or fifty pages. I'm either hooked or hating life. Yes, there's truth in the first chapter emphasis, but not every reader is like me. Most are nicer.

The first chapter needs to quickly establish a prominent tone, character, locale, or society. We went over this earlier when covering my rules on writing. Think of a kid tearing open a birthday present. They're so excited, and that wrapping paper you spent so much time on is ripped to shreds in seconds. They want the package underneath, the shiny, colorful box. With this concept in mind, you need to apply this to your first chapter in some capacity, reveal the package underneath.

Together, these two elements we discussed make a vow to the reader: this is worth the wait, this is worth your time and investment, but here's a little morsel to whet your appetite. So, yes, your first chapter is essential. Your first sentence? Not so much. Keep this in mind while crafting, but don't become entangled on your earlier drafts.

Doubt

I've been asked:

"Do you ever read your own writing and just think it's absolute garbage? Do you ever have moments where you feel like it sucks?"

The simple answer: yes. The longer answer: no. In the earlier days, I thought I knew everything, and my writing was a gift to the world. Beta readers and critiquers quickly disabused me of that foolish notion.

When I'm asked that question now, "do you think your writing sucks?" my answer is simple: "Every damn time I read it or conceive an idea."

The followup question that most people ask, which is the most important, "How do you push past it?" That is a little harder to answer because it's different for everyone. I can't show you that path. You'll have to find your method on your own, but I can tell you what I do.

"How do you push past it?" I don't. It haunts me every time. So, I just write and put it out of mind, turn inward on the plot elements and characters, and rely on beta readers to be honest. I hone my story through countless revisions, adding nuance to small plot elements, little twists and kernels of the past like droplets of water in a desert. I keep crafting long after the point I think something is good enough to share. Then I share, and I keep at it. I take the feedback I'm given, incorporate what's good, discard what isn't, and keep whittling, keep sculpting.

I once read a female author (I can't remember her name) answering this question on writer's block. She answered (paraphrasing), "I think about not eating, not paying the rent, my bills, and that gives me motivation, and the block is gone."

Everyone faces doubt, but you determine who is the master, it or you.

Chapter 7: Self-Editing

Self-Editing

The one thing most authors hate. Some of you may think or say, "But I don't know how to edit." We're going to go through what I do for every sentence in this chapter. You should always do this before sending out to editors, let alone your readers. You want to make their job easier, not harder.

For readers, you want to endear them to you and your story. They don't want to read convoluted, timey-wimey sentences. Your writing shouldn't detract from the incredible book you wrote. You should always strive to give a well-polished, tight-prosed, uncluttered canvas for editors to work with. By the end of this chapter, you'll have the tools necessary to go through your own work and do the same. Fair warning: like writing, editing is usually done in more than one go.

It's time to be ruthless. The gloves come off. This will be a brawl, a good ole fashioned slobber-knocker. We don't take prisoners, and we show no mercy. Mercy is weakness, and we want to cut all fragility from your manuscript. I hope you cry while we do this because it's hard, changes your brain as you evaluate the necessity for words.

If you've been editing your work for a while and read a book but start critiquing the prose, congratulations, you've turned yourself into a well-honed self-editor. I can never read a book without doing this now. Yes, it drove me mad for a few years, but I've learned to cope. If anything, it tells me the editor didn't do their job.

A quick insert about editors before getting to the self-editing. Each will be different. They will follow a particular set of grammar rules and ignore others. I'm old-fashioned, and I believe in the Oxford comma, and I will go down on that ship. Without the Oxford comma, the meaning of the sentence changes.

What is this Oxford madness of which you speak? A gross oversimplification: it's the second comma in a list of three. When you list things, you separate them with commas. However, in the last thirty-plus years, many writers and editors dropped it, but it's essential, and here's why.

If you are told to bring supplies to an art class, they don't say: "bring a canvas, brushes and oil." This doesn't make sense. A canvas isn't brushes and oil. Perhaps a weak example, but here's a better one. The valedictorian of your class is giving a speech in which he/she is thanking people.

"I'd like to thank my parents, Batman and Wonder Woman." The way this sentence is written, it's implied that the speaker is saying his/her parents are, in fact, Batman and Wonder Woman. How absurd is that notion? Instead, it should look like this: "I'd like to thank my parents, Batman, and Wonder Woman." Now, we've got a list of people, the parents, Batman, and Wonder Woman. This is the overall premise.

I digress.

Again, it's time to be ruthless. Know your editor and the rules they follow. If you have to fight for your comma, do so. In the end, it's your book, not theirs. They are there to help you polish your manuscript and make sure errors don't sneak past you.

Bottom line: listen to your editor, follow their advice, but choose the hills upon which you will die. If they tell you something isn't a grammar rule, challenge it.

But first, we must wade through our own editing phase, so let's dive in.

Adverbs

Stephen King is often quoted with the phrase, *"The road to hell is paved with adverbs."*

I agree.

Adverbs are not bad in themselves, and writers definitely need them from time to time. Did you see what I did there? I inserted an adverb, but my writing isn't littered with them. Using adverbs is a quick, easy insertion for modifying or describing something. Again, not all are bad if used in moderation. Let's take a look at that sentence just now.

Again, not all are bad if used in moderation.

We could've said, not all are bad if used sparingly. Not all are bad if used moderately, lightly, sparsely, thinly—point made. Now, imagine if every other line is filled with them. Not only is it repetitious and glaring, but it weakens the strength of your overall prose.

Relying on adverbs to do your heavy lifting is a crutch.

While I advocate for you to use the fewest words possible to get the meaning across in a clear manner, this is one of those times where the advice is wrong. Yes, an adverb can summarize something, but this doesn't mean it's better.

Take the dialogue tag, she said softly. Yes, you understand the gist of how, but can this be made better? How about, she said in a soft, breathy tone, or she said in a soft, anguished tone. To me, especially in dialogue tags, you want to be descriptive—if the moment calls for such. Not every tag needs to be. But if I had to choose between softly and said in a soft, anguished tone, I'll choose the latter every time.

Coupled with adverbs in dialogue tags is action beats. Adverbs after a word that already describes something weakens the first word. She slammed the door angrily. Well, if she's slamming the door, chances are it's done in anger, and we can tell this by what led up to the door being slammed. Adding angrily at the end is not only redundant but weakens the sentence. Instead of she slammed the door angrily, how about she slammed the door?

Another reason why they're bad is due to overuse. I've critiqued chapters for other writers, and in a two-thousand-word document, I find fifty-plus. You may not think this is a lot, but you'd be wrong. That comes out to about **one adverb for every forty words**, and if spaced as such, perhaps it wouldn't be so bad. Most of the time, they're clustered together. This also happens when you find repetition in words, which we'll discuss later in this chapter.

Bottom line: once you use one, it becomes easier to use another.

When I critique people's chapters, I highlight all the adverbs I noticed. Well, I highlight many things, but when they receive their chapter and note how many they're using, they cringe. I challenge you, open your chapter in a word doc or equivalent, and use the Find function. Type in (LY) How many hits did you get?

Yes, not all will be adverbs, but it'll help you navigate with efficiency. How many did you find? If the answer is twenty or less—depending on the word count—you're on the right track. If you got twenty out of six thousand words, I'd say you're good. That's **one for every three hundred words**. However, if you only have fifteen-hundred words and you've got twenty, it's time to be ruthless.

Go through and look at each. Ask yourself, 'is this necessary?' If the answer is no, cut, and that goes double if it's in a dialogue tag or action beat. Read your other sentences. Does the adverb help or detract from an otherwise strong sentence? Take a razor to them. The challenge is straight forward. Go through and cut out half. If you find fifty, shoot for twenty-five.

Did you do it? Good. Was it easy? Perhaps, perhaps not. Now, go again. I want you to try your hardest to half the number. Do I expect you to manage it? Yes and no. If you got them down to fifteen, I would applaud you.

Just a side note: don't count words ending with an 'ly' if they aren't an adverb, like early.

"In the early morning, we'll set out on the trail." But you could say 'wee' if you want.

Key takeaway: Adverbs aren't your friend; they weaken your writing, so—cut, cut, cut.

Remember: self-editing is about being ruthless. Show no mercy to your manuscript or yourself.

Filler Words

What is a filler word? In short, it's a word that holds little to no meaning. In essence, you can take the word out, and it doesn't alter the sentence in the slightest. There are more than the words I'll list, but these are the most notorious, not only in my writing, but in everyone's I've read, including published authors.

One thing to note: not all of them can be cut out, nor should you try. Some are a necessity, and there's no way around them. This is okay. We want to cut the ones with no value to the prose itself, not take out a pivotal word in a carefully constructed line.

The list: *that, just, even, seem, very*, and *really*.

In the case of a character responding to someone by saying 'really?', we wouldn't cut this one. But we can cut from a sentence like this: "It's really important." Why not, "it's important?" Let's try some other sentences and clean up the clutter.

"Today was a very bad day."

We can trim here.

"Today was bad."

Not only did we cut out the redundant day, but we took out very. To be fair, it's a weak line overall. If you want to insist the day was more than bad, we need to use a stronger word.

"Today was atrocious/ terrible/ a slog."

Utilizing these stronger words, we get the same meaning across, if not more so, and we cut filler words. We are getting ahead of ourselves on *word choice* here, which will be covered in the next section. Let's navigate back to filler words.

"I understand that, but can't you see that is preposterous?"

What's wrong with the sentence above, other than it won't win any prose awards? We used 'that' twice; one isn't necessary, and the other can be condensed to a contraction. We'll try it now.

> *"I understand, but can't you see that's preposterous?"*

Now, onto another.

> *"Yes, I can see, but you just don't seem to understand how very important this decision is."*

How can we clean this up? There's more than a few filler words within. How about …

> *"Yes, I can see, but you don't understand how important this decision is."*

Again, you can go in with word choice and emphasize *how* important it is. Since we are talking about word choice, we're going to jump to that topic now.

Word Choice

From the previous section, we have this dialogue going:

> *"I understand, but can't you see that's preposterous?"*
> *"Yes, I can, but you don't understand how important this decision is."*

We already cleared out the 'very' in front of the word important. As stated before, we can bolster *how* important by using word choice.

> *"Yes, I can, but you don't understand how pivotal this decision is."*
> *"Yes, I can, but you don't understand how paramount this decision is."*
> *"Yes, I can, but you don't understand how crucial this decision is."*

We've got options to play with here. You can use any type of word to change the meaning of the sentence or enhance the decision by the selection we make. In the last line, we used crucial. What if we took it out and inserted comical? How does this change the sentence? Quite drastically.

Word choice is all about taking these smaller, broad, general words and choosing a better one. Instead of saying large, we can pick colossal, massive, gigantic, you get the picture. But we must also be careful with what word we select because it can change the meaning of the sentence and the tone of the scene.

If we chose another word that technically meant large but not in the context we wanted, it'd sound off or alter the meaning. Other words that mean large in different contexts are excessive, abundant, hefty, boundless. If you're describing a large monster, you don't want to say, "It had boundless legs." No, we'd want to say, "It had massive legs."

Storytime: In one of my earliest drafts of my first book, *The Bearer of Secrets*, I used a modern word to describe an object. Though that may not seem like an issue, my world was set in a medieval times, castles and dragons and warriors with swords. So, what's the problem? Setting the locale aside, I wanted to describe the color of the stone in a wall, and I couldn't think of how to say it in terms matching what I envisioned, so I inserted the modern term and went on. The person who was reading for me ran across it, and … well, not only laughed but talked about how it pulled him out of the story.

So, what's the word?

I described the wall as fire-truck red. As you can see, this would be detrimental not only to the story but the reader. Using words or phrases of our modern world set in a story that wouldn't have these things can be a distraction. I would almost argue it's less suitable to use a modern word in a story set in ancient times than an everyday term used in futuristic novels. Theoretically, folks from the future would know what an anvil is compared to a cleric knowing what fire-truck red is.

I digress.

Bottom line: word choice is crucial, so be careful when selecting your alternatives. And yes, when editing, this means going line by line and asking yourself, is this the best word?

Remember: on your first or third draft, it's more important to get the story down on paper rather than worrying if it's the right word or not. Leave some for the editing.

So, like the filler words, there are generic words with vague or little meaning: big, small, little, tiny; these give you a vague idea of the size but not in exacting measurements. Select with care.

Let's move on.

Initial Conjunctions

Initial conjunctions aren't all bad, despite what your elementary school teacher may have told you. People use initial conjunctions while speaking, and if you want to be accurate, especially in your dialogue, you've got to tell yourself it's okay to use them. Having said this, you don't want to overuse them, much like the repetition of words. More on that later.

What are the initial conjunctions? Well, for this segment, I'm talking about the short list. Yes, there's a longer list, but I'm discussing FANBOYS: for, and, nor, but, or, yet, and so. It's okay to use these as sentence starters in moderation. But if every other sentence is starting with one, you need to do a heavy-handed edit. Not only that, each time someone reads them, it should be like a breath of fresh air and not the fart-recycled airplane type. They can help break up the monotony of your prose, so this invaluable tool should be in your toolbelt. Right, Batman?

> **Storytime:** David, a friend of mine, never realized how much he used initial conjunctions until he got a few critiques from me. There were numerous green highlights, and since it was a visual representation of the issue, it had a profound impact. When I critique him

now, I've got to hunt for those. This is a positive change.

In fact, he might be a little too ruthless when cutting, and I might find three in his entire chapter. Again, moderation is vital; overuse is terrible; but too little? Could this be negative? You decide. What's best for you and your story?

Remember: writing is a delicate balance of a lot of moving parts. You've got to find your rhythm, and that will only come with time. Let's tackle repetition next.

Repetition & Generic Words

Repetition was my bane for many years, and it plagues new authors and aficionados alike. Do you remember the segment in which I used only five-word sentences for a whole paragraph? Rather monotonous, right? You should try writing something like that sometime. It's tedious. Anyway, repetition is much like the five-word sentences and it grates the nerves. When I see this in published works, I either think the editor didn't do their job by pointing this out, or the author lacks an imagination. Or perhaps, we're reading their first draft, and they never went back to fix.

So, what do I mean by repetition? Well, in this book, I've used some good repetition and some bad. Let's take the word repetition. How many times have I used that particular word in this section alone? Go back up and count.

I counted five so far. Now, the question we should ask: is this good or bad? To be honest, that depends. If I try to write by avoiding the word, I'll be writing in circles or dancing around. This can be tedious for your reader. But we're specifically talking about repetition, and there's no way to avoid the word as it's our subject. We can, however, use moderation. Where possible, we can use a different word like repeating, reiteration, and the like.

So, as of now, in this particular section, I wouldn't say it's a bad thing. When we counted, we had five, but what if we had a higher number like thirteen? I'd say it's terrible since we were only two paragraphs in. So, when does it become detrimental, and when is it okay? That's an age-old question without a magic formula to tell us. It's something intuitive.

For me, when I go through and edit my work, I try to whittle specific word repetition down to about eight per chapter depending on word count and the word itself. If the chapter is only fifteen hundred words, I might cut more. If my chapter is fourteen thousand words, I'll go a little easier on my "hard eight" rule.

Now, this is difficult, especially when utilizing words without an equivalent—case in point: the word wand. We really don't have many options for this word. You could use other words like a stick, but it's not the same. You could say weapon, and while true, it doesn't ring with the clarity we need.

In the world of Ermaeyth in *The Bearer of Secrets*, people fight and die by the sword. Is there another word we can use for a sword? Absolutely. We can use the actual type of sword like a rapier or a hand-and-a-half, but we can use other words like edge, steel, blade, saber, and we can also use words to imply what we're talking about. If you know they've got a sword, you can say, he stabbed his opponent, you don't need to say, "he stabbed him with the sword." Again, unnecessary repetition.

There's another type of repeating we need to discuss, and this has more to do with a singular word clustered around a small area. Sometimes, we have a tendency to use a word within a sentence, within a few sentences of each other, or paragraphs. We also want to cut this if possible.

> *"We caught an assassin, my lord."*
> *"Assassin? Where's the assassin? Who sent them?"*
> *"We haven't interrogated him yet, but we'll get the answers soon enough."*
> *"Where did you capture the assassin? Here? In the castle?"*

Okay, again, a very generic exchange, but the point is made. We can cut out many of the assassin words within. Let's try now.

> *"We caught an assassin, my lord."*
> *"Assassin? Where? Who sent them?"*
> *"We haven't interrogated him yet, but we'll get the answers soon enough."*
> *"Where did you capture him? Here? In the castle?"*

We were able to remove one that was nothing more than repeating, and we replaced the other by using the gender of the individual. Not bad.

We went from four to two. While this word stands out, others don't, like generic terms such as look/looked. These tend to blend in with the words around them, and you don't notice them until you read that everyone is looking around.

> He looked at her. She lifted her eyes to meet his, then he looked away. Off in the distance, he saw a dozen men on horses following them. He looked back at her.
> "We've got company."
> "Still?"
> "Look for yourself."

There's a lot of looking going on. Many people don't realize they're using something as simple as this generic word because of its ability to blend in. What other words can be used here? Also, while going strong, let's try to tighten the prose and cut out the unnecessary.

> He glanced at her. She lifted her eyes to his, then he turned away. Off in the distance, a dozen men on horses followed them. He looked back at her.
> "We've got company."
> "Still?"
> "See for yourself."

Again, the example isn't an award winner, but it's not meant to be. We're here to learn how to make the bland better. So, do you have an issue with repetition in your writing? The generic words or specific ones like wands, swords, or assassins? This is a lot to remember, but editing is line by line, and you've got as much time as you need to fix any issue.

Capitalization

When we are writing a story set in our incredible, fictitious world, we have a tendency to want to make it more memorable. And how do we do that? We capitalize everything in sight! This gets caps, and that gets caps, caps for everybody!

This isn't as awesome as you think.

First, if everything gets capitalization, nothing is unique. So, why are we capitalizing in the first place? If you are big on caps, make a list of everything you want to push in the uppercase sphere and start crossing

111

out anything that's not significant. When you've narrowed down the list to three items or so, there's wiggle room.

Second, even though we are visiting your fantasy world, you should still follow Earth's grammar rules. A lot of us have misconceptions about proper grammar, myself included. Titles, for instance, come to mind. Here's a quick and dirty way to remember this rule. Let's say we're aboard the Millennium Falcon, and Han Solo is our captain. Let's take a look at titles for both direct and indirect use.

Ex: 1
"There goes the captain again, always complaining
        stuff is broken."

Ex: 2
"Who's that?"
"Oh, that's the boss, Captain Han Solo."

Direct vs. indirect. The same goes for kings, queens, presidents, leaders, military, dignitaries, ambassadors, and parents.

Ex: 3
"Who's that?"
"My father."

Ex: 4
"Hello, Mother. How was your day?"

Why am I going over this? It's simple. You have many things you *need* to capitalize, so why add more to the never-ending list? Also, you need to remember it throughout your first book, your second, and the entire series.

This brings me to my next point: races. Elves and dwarves are not capitalized. We don't capitalize human, so why would we for these races? Is there a good time to capitalize something?

Yes.

In my first book, *The Bearer of Secrets*, I cap one specific group, the Krey. Why did I do this? In a sprawling tale with so many races, people, places, and unique things, I wanted them to stand out so the reader would be reminded on a subconscious level of who they are. Seeing the Krey in the middle of a long sentence talking about other things is a great way to emphasize the importance.

112

So, is there something unique in your book you want to show as significant? Be selective in your decision. Moving on.

What if a word has more than one meaning in your book, and you want to distinguish the two? There's an excellent tool for text called italics, and we use this to stress words in a sentence. This can be utilized in those instances instead of caps. If your monk prays to the gods, but *prays* to cast a spell, using italics gets the point across rather than going the uppercase route. When you reread and go through edits, if you do the upper and lowercase, each time you run across one or the other, you need to read for context to determine if you used the right one.

Bottom line: half of your book doesn't need to be capitalized. Go easy on yourself, and your reader will thank you, too. I'm not advocating you can't ever capitalize; I'm saying be selective. Trust your reader.

Pronouns

Pronouns can both save and destroy your writing. Have you ever read something replete with he and she or his and her? How many of those do you think can be cut? I imagine a lot. Whether amateur, self-published, or through a publishing house, pronouns plague all walks of writing. Most of the time, these pronouns are invisible to us, and if that's the case, this is excellent news for your writing. However, redundancy rears its ugly head, and we notice. So, let's cut as many as we can.

> Ex: 1. She opened the door, stepped through, and closed it behind her. Giving the room a cursory glance, she waded forward, tossed her keys on her table, and moved deeper into the room. A small smile spread across her lips. No one was home. Finally, a little peace and quiet.

What's wrong with the example above? Technically? Nothing. Again, the prose isn't worthy of a Pulitzer, but they're not meant to be. But there's redundancy within the segment, and we can trim the brisket fat from beneath. Let's try it now.

> Ex: 2. She opened the door, stepped through, and closed it. Giving the room a cursory glance, she waded forward and tossed the keys on the table. A small smile

spread across her lips. No one was home.
Finally, a little peace and quiet.

This edit blends with overall editing, cutting out unnecessary words but also slicing pronouns. Let's go line by line so you can note why I made the choices.

> She opened the door, stepped through, and closed it behind her.

I cut out 'behind her' because if you step through a doorway, it's behind you. Second, we know it's her because we started the sentence with 'she.' The only thing we need to determine at this point is if she closed the door.

> Giving the room a cursory glance, she waded forward, tossed her keys on her table, and moved deeper into the room.

Okay, three pronouns in this sentence. You face a decision to cut one or two of them or none. I'm pretty ruthless, so I cut two of them. Instead of tossing her keys on her table, we replace both 'hers' with 'the.'

If, in your book, you've established this location as her home, there's no point in saying it's her table later on. If it's the first time, then you might want to specify. I mean, what if it's the neighbor's house? Well, hopefully, you've set that up before she entered the premises. So, you can still get away with 'on the table.' But the keys? Are they hers or the neighbor's? That takes a few words before entry.

Moving to the next part, I cut "and moved deeper into the room." That's just authorial preference. Earlier in the sentence, she waded forward, implying she's moving away from the door and into the room proper. In this case, this is redundant, so why repeat it? I cut this segment, as the progression is implied.

And the last bit:

> A small smile spread across her lips. No one was home. Finally, a little peace and quiet.

From both examples above, this stayed the same as nothing was worth cutting. Since we cut out the first two 'hers,' this last one could stay, and it's needed to signify whose lips are smiling. Otherwise, there's nothing to change here.

Okay, now that we've gone through this, I hope you understand what's going through my head when I read something I've written, and why I make cuts. Self-editing requires ruthlessness. We're here to make your prose shine. The major edits should always come from you, not your editors. Granted, they have a job to do, but you should ease their burden, and that'll endear you to them. But not everyone can hire a team of editors, so you need to do the legwork yourself. Scrutinize every line, every word. We'll talk more about editors later in the chapter.

Practice Editing

For this segment, I'm going to state at the beginning that we'll be employing the Fair Use doctrine. In United States copyright law, fair use is a doctrine that permits limited use of copyrighted material without acquiring permission from the rights holders. Examples of fair use include commentary, criticism, and teaching. Since this book is indeed teaching, and we'll be commenting and critiquing, I think it'd be prudent to annotate this at the beginning of this section.

Also, I want to make it clear that I'm not ripping on this author. I think the premise of her story is amazing, and I wish I had thought it up.

Now, on to editing.

This first excerpt is from a published author, Laurell K. Hamilton. This is pulled from her book *Bloody Bones*.

Learning all we have from this chapter, we're going to edit this in our own authorial voice. Read it, ponder where she excelled and where you think it can be improved. Try to edit it yourself. What would you do differently? What would you keep the same?

> "What's wolf-boy in the back going to do?"
> "I do what I'm told," Jason said.
> "Great," I said.
> We drove in silence. Jean-Claude rarely sweats small talk, and I wasn't in the mood. We could all have a nice little visit, but out there somewhere Jeff Quinlan had woken to a second night in Xavier's tender care. Sort of ruined the mood for me.

115

"The turn is just ahead to your right, ma petite." Jean-Claude's voice made me jump. I had sunk into the silence and the dark hush of the highway.

I slowed the Jeep. Didn't want to miss the turnoff. A gravel road, like a hundred other gravel roads, spilled off the main road. There was nothing to make it stand out. Nothing special. The road was narrow with trees growing so close on either side it was like driving through a tunnel. The naked branches of trees curved around us like interlocking pieces of a wall. The headlights slid over the nearly naked trees, bouncing when the Jeep eased over a pothole. Naked wooden fingers tapped the roof of the Jeep. It was damn near claustrophobic.

Source: Laurell K. Hamilton: Bloody Bones: An Anita Blake, Vampire Hunter Novel (pp. 180-181). Penguin Publishing Group. Kindle Edition.

Okay, so, where do you land? Did you try to edit it? Did it read well before you started? What, if anything, would you change? How about after you edited it? So, in the vein of sharing my thoughts on editing, I did this exercise, too, and will share below.

"What's wolf-boy in the back going to do?"

"I do what I'm told," Jason mumbled.

"Great," I said.

We drove in brittle silence. Jean-Claude never cared for small talk, and I wasn't in the mood, not when Jeff Quinlan was suffering Xavier's tender care for a second night. My mood soured at the thought. I was glad that I didn't have an excuse to bring down the rest of the group. Sort of ruined the mood for me.

"The turn is just ahead to your right, ma petite." Jean-Claude's voice made me jump. I had grown accustomed to the silence and the rhythmic hum of the highway.

I slowed the Jeep. Good thing, too. I almost missed the turn-off. The lane looked like any of a hundred other gravel roads, and the dark night obscured the path. Nothing made it stand out.

The narrow road was hedged with encroaching trees, reminding me of driving through a tunnel. The branches curved around us like curled, interlocking fingers. The headlights slid over the winter-bare trunks, bouncing when the Jeep eased over a pothole. Splayed wooden hooks tapped the roof of the Jeep. It was damn near claustrophobic.

Original Source: Laurell K. Hamilton: Bloody Bones: An Anita Blake, Vampire Hunter Novel (pp. 180-181). Penguin Publishing Group. Kindle Edition.

Now that you've seen what I've done with the small passage, what was better? What was worse?

Remember: in editing—as in writing—you have your authorial voice, and this is where you distinguish yourself. Everyone has their unique style; how is yours different? Are you a copycat? Do you want to write like J. K. Rowling or George R. R. Martin? It's great to emulate, but in this instance, don't be a carbon copy.

Without bogging down this segment of the book, I've decided to skip using more works and editing and move on. My challenge to you is to go back and read other people's works, whether just a page or a paragraph, and see where you can make improvements. What can you cut? What can you alter? What's a better word choice? Did you spot any filler words or repetition? Any initial conjunctions?

Let's move on to the last section of this chapter: editors.

Get an Editor

At the beginning of the book, I said I wasn't going to cover agent hunting and publishing, but a beta reader told me I should add a little in about editors. So, taking the suggestion, we'll discuss it.

Everything we've gone over in this chapter are things *you* should do *before* submitting your work to an editor. They help you shine, fix fatal flaws, clarify technicalities, bolster your grammar by removing errors, but they don't write your novel for you. That falls on you. When they come back with suggestions and fixes, guess who's going to make the ultimate decision and fix it? You.

I won't profess to be an expert authority on editors. I'm not one, nor have I worked in the field, but I can tell you what I know, and the first is the most important. There are multiple to choose from.

Most people start with a developmental editor. They look at your story as a whole (character arc, setting, plot, etc.), the overarching portions of your work. They earn the big bucks for a reason: to help you create a stronger story, characters, and world.

Then you move on to line editing. These folks make sure your story reads well, focusing on sentence structure, description, and making sure the character is still blonde from page one to the end, etc. Some developmental editors do line editing too.

When I edit my work, this is the one I fall under for the most part. I do tend to be a blend of line and copy editing. This is also how I give feedback—line by line. Those who've received a critique from me will see a plethora of comments, suggestions, fixes, strike-throughs, and highlights. Their first inclination is "Man, this guy hates my writing! What a jerk!" But that's far from the case.

Remember: like editors, critiquers are just as varied, so keep this in mind.

Next is copy editing, focusing on grammar, syntax, punctuation, etc. Hopefully, this person knows all the rules you can break and which can be bent. Just because this particular copy editor "studied the rules" doesn't mean they're following the same ones as the person two businesses over. Each is different with an emphasis on what something means to them. There isn't a measuring stick they all live by.

Taking this analogy of a ruler, all rulers measure distance. Some are made of wood, others are plastic, and some metal. They can measure in the metric or in the standard units. Though they accomplish the same goals, in the end, all are different. Don't forget this when seeking out a copy editor.

Last is proofreading and *must* be done with nothing else left to do. They make sure everything's in its place from chapter headings, page numbers, etc. If you add or remove scenes after a proofreader has gone through the manuscript, you will have wasted your money. Be sure of your final product before you tackle this last segment.

A word of caution: If your friend has a degree in English or some other equivalent, that's great, but that doesn't mean they're a professional —especially if they don't use it daily in the industry. Think of your book as a patient about to go in for a heart transplant. Do you want the doctor who studied hard and made 100's on his exams and practical applications, performed his residency with flawless acclaim, or do you want the doctor who passed by the skin of his teeth, drank until they passed out every night and stumbled to a Ph.D.?

I know who I'd pick.

Applying this scenario to your book, do you want the professional who lives and breathes grammar or the one who has a piece of paper that says they earned their degree? That's not to say your friend made terrible grades, but one of these is a pro who does this for a living, and the other doesn't. You decide. Choose wisely.

Lessons learned over time: Everyone is a pro with their opinions and pass such off as gospel. I can't tell you how many times I've heard, "You should let me edit for you. I know what I'm talking about." When this gets tossed my way, I say, "Thank you; I'll take it under advisement." Most of the time, I ask them to point out what they're talking about, and they can't or won't.

When wading into the realm of editors, I urge unrestrained caution. What people see as a mistake may be something not aligned with their preference. If anything, I'd be inclined to use these folks as a beta reader. You can never have enough eyes on your work before you publish.

As I told my editor when we first started working together all those years ago: I want to be right. This is a battle between my authorial voice and my desire to be correct. And yes, I'm a bit OCD and a perfectionist while crafting a story, characters, and writing. I obsess over every detail. I drove my poor editor crazy with incessant questions and comments. If she didn't sport gray hair before—she does now.

In the end, this is your work of art, and yes, it is art. Writing is art. It's a blend of every element within this book and more. You've taken time out of your life, perhaps years, sacrificed late nights, shows, hanging out with friends, sweated every detail, cried out in frustration, and agonized over every line. If you haven't, hold off on the editing. You may need to review your work some more.

So, jot your story down. Write it, write again, and again. Go through as many versions as you need. Then edit, edit, edit. Whittle, chisel, and sculpt. As the saying goes, you can't edit a blank page, and you can't see the statue beneath the slab of marble until you start chiseling. Think of it this way, writing is planting a seed to a tree, and with each character, chapter, and revision, it's growing into a massive cypress. When self-editing, we are taking a chain saw and shears to prune the tree into something beautiful without all the hanging limbs and twisted branches.

Chapter 8: Extras and Closing

Lessons Learned Over the Years

Pleasing Everyone: You won't. It's impossible. Take everything, both good and bad, with a grain of salt and sometimes a spoonful of sugar.

Generic Words: See, saw, look, looked, looking, felt, feel, even, just, wanted, really, big, large, small. Get rid of them and break out your thesaurus. Use a stronger word that brings more clarity.

Empty/Filler Words: just, that, even, really, only, very, still. You can't get rid of them all, but you can try. If it's not a keyword within the sentence where its absence would change the meaning, cut it.

Silence:

> **Storytime**: So once, when I paid for an edit way back in the day, an editor told me that when an author uses something along the lines of "They sat in silence for a few minutes, they waited for a while, ... etc." that the author has grown bored with the passage. I don't know if this is true of you, and I wouldn't presume, but I would suggest you reevaluate your scene if you've used this phrase and see if it's true. In fact, when you use silence, this may be a perfect time to go into an introspective look of your character.

Interruptions: When there is an interruption, use an emdash—the long line just like we did now.

Felt: Try to veer away from telling words like felt. It cannot be helped all the time, but in this case, it probably can. Don't tell us they're feeling, just say it. Instead of "she felt the sadness forming in her heart," say, "sadness formed in her heart."

Began To:

> **Storytime**: An editor once told me, whenever you can, drop any "began to" and "started to" as it is the mark of an amateur writer. In the same breath, she said that it cannot always be helped, but when you can, cut, cut, cut. Opinion: To me, when I read it—since the editor told

me—it sticks out like a sore thumb. It's evident in pro-writers, too.

Remember: you can use it, just do so sparingly—like adverbs. Practice writing your sentences without these helping words.

Capitalizations: When speaking directly to folks and using their rank, title, or honorific, they're uppercase. When talking about those people in an indirect way, e.g., not to their face, go with lower. It's a quick and dirty rule, but that's the gist of it.

Lowercasing: Consider using lowercase where applicable. In fantasy, you make up many of your own rules, but once you start, you can never stop, no matter how many books you write. I know that I capitalize on specific things, too, so this isn't a knock on you for doing the same; however, I recommend simplifying where you can.

The use of very: "Substitute 'damn' every time you're inclined to write 'very;' your editor will delete it, and the writing will be just as it should be." — Mark Twain

Adverbs: I'm not advocating that all adverbs are wrong to use; however, as Stephen King once said, "The pathway to hell is paved with adverbs."

Quotes to Write By

1.   There's no wrong or right way to write.
2.   You can never go wrong with investing in yourself.
3.   Set up the scene with the fewest number of words possible while painting a vivid picture. Spare no expense in the detail, but sacrifice the lengthy prose on the altar of precision.
4.   Write for you, but edit for your readers.
5.   I'm old-fashioned, and I believe in the Oxford comma, and I will go down on that ship.
6.   When I do world-build a specific element of my story, I drill it down to the gritty details, then summarize the whole thing, and try to cut ninety percent when I insert.
7.   I've often found when writing—and reading other people's stories—the more introspective you go in a character's head, the slower the pace becomes for the reader. You must augment this with some form of action, or at the very least, progress.

8. Selecting a target audience comes with a mindset. It will change not only your prose, theme, and content, but mold you as a writer as well.

9. If you're writing a series or a trilogy, you don't have to relay *everything* to your reader up front. You've got time to peel it back in layers.

10. Failure is the backbone of success, in every walk of life. So, fail. Fail many times. Hit rock bottom, but pick yourself up, and try again.

11. Limit distractions.

12. Think of a kid tearing open a birthday present. They're so excited, and that wrapping paper you spent so much time on is ripped to shreds in seconds. They want the package underneath, the shiny, colorful box. With this concept in mind, you need to apply this to your first chapter in some capacity, reveal the package underneath.

13. Listen to your editor, follow their advice, but choose the hills upon which you will die.

14. The more specific you get in elements of your story, i.e. moving further away from a general audience, the smaller your reading circle will be.

15. Great writing comes with the revisions.

16. Whenever possible, eliminate dialogue tags.

17. If you find something that works for you, stick with it.

18. Writing time is precious, so don't waste it on things that won't make the book or impact the story.

19. It's okay if your readers have questions left unanswered at the end of a book.

20. You don't have to have all the answers before your write.

21. Character over plot wins every time.

22. You may not be able to build a world like Pandora in *Avatar*, or have the vision of George Lucas to create the next *Star Wars*, but you can craft the next Ellen Ripley or Samwise Gamgee.

23. The key takeaway from the dialogue section is the blend of said, other dialogue tags, action beats, and internal emotions and thoughts.

24. Action and tension go hand in hand.

25. "The path to hell is paved with adverbs."—Stephen King

26. Don't worry about your first draft. Just get it down on paper.

27. How many people do you know read the first sentence of a book and say, "Well, that sucked," and then put the book down? I've never met a single soul who confesses to this.

28. Your first chapter is important. Your first sentence? Not so much.

29. Your first chapter, and your first sentence, together, make a vow to the reader: this is worth the wait, this is worth your time and investment, but here's a little morsel to whet your appetite.

30. Self-editing is about being ruthless. Show no mercy to your manuscript or yourself.

31. Take out filler or mostly useless words like *that, just, even, seem, very*, and *really*. Not every one of them can be removed but cut 98% of them.

32. Avoid info dumps.

33. There's a stark difference between writing a book that happens to have a theme, and using your book as a vehicle to preach.

34. Risk your characters. Most folks in their stories have plot armor, whether visible or not.

35. Whether villain or hero, characters make or break a story. No one sees themselves as a sidekick. They're the protagonist of their own story.

36. Characters are more than their looks, they are more than a role they fill in a story. They aren't defined by a singular trait such as appearance, what group they identify with, where they were born, or sexuality. They're people, and we've got to view them as such.

37. As Bob Ross said with painting, so it is true with writing: "You have an artistic license."

38. Remember: writing is a delicate balance of a lot of moving parts. You've got to find your rhythm, and that will only come with time.

39. The end goal should be, to learn, to evolve, to become more, and to write an awesome story with amazing characters.

40. To me, the hair color, eye color, and ethnicity are trivial matters in the grand scheme. These aspects I decide almost last unless I'm building a particular character or race from a segment of my world. That's the exterior packaging which is minimal to the depth of the character. They base themselves on their beliefs, moral code, motivation, internal desires, and the traits they embody.

41. "Substitute 'damn' every time you're inclined to write 'very;' your editor will delete it and the writing will be just as it should be." — Mark Twain

42. Everyone faces doubt, but you determine who is the master, it or you.

Zodiacs

Aries
Positive: Adventurous and energetic, pioneering and courageous, enthusiastic and confident, dynamic and quick-witted

Negative: Selfish, quick-tempered, impulsive, impatient, foolhardy, and reckless.

Taurus
Positive: Patient, reliable, warmhearted, loving, persistent, determined, placid, security loving

Negative: Jealous, possessive, resentful, inflexible, self-indulgent, greedy

Gemini
Positive: adaptable, versatile, communicative, witty, intellectual, eloquent, youthful, lively

Negative: nervous, tense, superficial, inconsistent, cunning, inquisitive.

Cancer
Positive: emotional, loving, intuitive, imaginative, shrewd, cautious, protective, sympathetic

Negative: changeable, moody, overemotional, touchy, clinging—unable to let go.

Leo

Positive: generous, warmhearted, creative, enthusiastic, broad-minded, expansive, faithful, loving
Negative: pompous, patronizing, bossy, interfering, dogmatic, intolerant.

Virgo
Positive: modest, shy, meticulous, reliable, practical, diligent, intelligent, analytical
Negative: fussy, worry-prone, overcritical, harsh, perfectionistic, rigid.

Libra
Positive: diplomatic, urbane, romantic, charming, easygoing, sociable, idealistic, peaceable
Negative: indecisive, changeable, gullible, easily influenced, flirtatious, self-indulgent

Scorpio
Positive: determined, forceful, emotional, intuitive, powerful, passionate, exciting, magnetic
Negative: jealous, resentful, compulsive, obsessive, secretive, obstinate.

Sagittarius
Positive: optimistic, freedom-loving, jovial, good-humored, honest, straightforward, intellectual, philosophical.
Negative: blindly optimistic, careless, irresponsible, superficial, tactless, restless

Capricorn
Positive: practical, prudent, ambitious, disciplined, patient, careful, humorous, reserved
Negative: Pessimistic, fatalistic, miserable, grudging

Aquarius
Positive: friendly, humanitarian, honest, loyal, original, inventive, independent, intellectual
Negative: intractable, contrary, perverse, unpredictable, unemotional, detached

Pisces

Positive: imaginative, sensitive, compassionate, kind, selfless, unworldly, intuitive, sympathetic

Negative: escapist, idealistic, secretive, vague, weak-willed, easily led

30 Character Motivations

Addiction, Atonement, Avoidance,
Death Wish, Debt Repayment, Denial,
Desire, Duty, Escapism
Fame/Infamy, Fear, Freedom,
Glory, Greed, Guilt,
Honor, Justice, Love,
Loyalty, Morality, Notoriety,
Obedience, Obsession, Paranoia,
Power, Redemption, Regret,
Revenge, Shame, Survival

Final Thoughts & Summary

I hope this book has been informative and helps you deep-dive characters, or at the very least, give you a new way to look at characters, build them, and flesh out elements of story and writing.

Quick recap of my methods for the road:
Know what type of writer you are. What is your strength?
Set the mood with music.
Don't waste excessive amounts of time on world building.
Build characters from the inside out, start with the zodiac as the basis.

Write down your tent poles for the book or the series; know where you are headed, but the journey should be as much as a surprise to you as the reader.

When you get stuck on a plot point, there are three questions you need to ask yourself.

1: What is the most logical outcome?

2: What would I or my characters like to see happen?

3: How can I turn this on its head, go completely left field, and still deliver a believable and fascinating story?

When you've written your manuscript, let it sit for a while before going back through.

Once you've written it a few times, now it's time to self edit: Whittle, chisel, and sculpt.

Bottom line from this entire book: take what works for you and stick with it. If you find something that doesn't fit your writing style, don't discard—just file it away for later. You never know when the next opportunity to utilize these tools will come knocking.

Help lift other writers up. If you see them struggling with something you've gone through, show them the way. Build them up, not tear them down. Treat them as you'd want to be treated. You'll knock months or years off their writing with well-placed advice. They'll become a stronger author because of it. We want better books out there, and faster, too.

Find your writing rules, create them, and let them guide you. Discover your words to live by. What author or icon said something that clarified and gave meaning to your struggle? What writing tools can aid you? Keep your focus, make time, and pace yourself. As Bob Ross used to say, "We don't make mistakes, we have happy accidents." Nothing you do in your journey to becoming the best writer you can be is a mistake.

And finally, always remember, "There's no wrong or right way to write."

About the Author

Kyle Belote is a prior active-duty Marine, writer, musician, and painter. He's lived in Texas, Hawaii, and Okinawa, Japan, and has traveled the globe. When not writing, he enjoys sketching, researching companies and investing, and reading and listening to audiobooks. Kyle enjoys a diverse collection of films, books, and shows—just not the abomination called Disney Star Wars.

For more information, please visit: www.outpostdire.com

Back Jacket

Characters forged in blood, flaws, and consequence don't come from formulas. Craft unforgettable heroes like Ellen Ripley or Samwise Gamgee with Flawed to the Core.

Fantasy and sci-fi author Kyle Belote, renowned for gritty characters and morally complex tales, reveals his raw, unflinching approach to character creation. Beneath the polite layers of storytelling lies his practical method for building authentic, flawed protagonists. Discover tools for immersive worlds, compelling scenes, and gripping twists—from dialogue and action to self-editing and tastefully written intimacy.

Whether starting your first draft or bleeding into the fifth, this book is your scalpel and shield. Don't write safe stories. Create true ones.

www.ingramcontent.com/pod-product-compliance
Lightning Source LLC
LaVergne TN
LVHW091308080426
835510LV00007B/413